TRUST
THE
PROCESS

Reflections of a Nonprofit
Race Equity Movement

DR. MICHELLE MAJORS

Dedicated to my friends at Columbia Legal Services, but especially The Collective.

Thank you.

Contents

One More River

Wide was the river we crossed from slavery
scarred backs, proud chests, acts of bravery

We packed just a little more than pride
for the Underground Railroad ride
the whole while singing, "We Exalt Thee"

Only faith could have helped us cross the cold waters
when we knew the sure punishment was slaughter

Slipped. Sneaked. Prayed for salvation from every station
until Juneteenth and the promise of emancipation-
the long awaited freedom for our sons and our daughters

Then came the time we got to know a formidable foe:
a slanky fellow by the name Jim Crow
who did legislate the rapids of the river to flow against us
and marked the moment when our people learned not to trust
the nation, nor the scale, or which direction the river flowed

Lord sent a King to teach us how to fight
in ways that were civilized for our Civil Rights
We learned to sit, walk, and march with compassion
against those who held a stake in the profit of oppression
held on to their power and privilege with all their might

the river's rapids are rough, but the water does still flow
for this renewed fight against brutality
for the continued struggle for equality and equity
in the workplace and beyond and the places we don't yet know
We choose to cross this river to a new plateau

Talena Lachelle Queen

Foreword

More than 100 years have passed since W. E. B. Du Bois coined the phrase, "color line" to describe the problems of the 20th century. Today, the problem of the 21st century remains the color line. How does one write about lawyers who fight against the injustices on the most vulnerable while grappling with their own privilege and attitudes that perpetuate the very system they claim to oppose? Not only does Michelle Majors celebrate the applauded efforts of one law firm's work to create workplace equity, she also includes steps for organizations who choose to take on the necessary task of creating a workplace culture of belonging, inclusion, and equity,

Workplace of belonging

One of the brightest illustrations of the "color line" is the unwritten, but closely adhered to idea of who belongs where. Countless examples throughout history can be denoted here: consider who is allowed to swim at the public pools, sit in front of the bus, walk in certain neighborhoods or, in contemporary times, who is allowed to have barbeques at the park or attend yoga classes. For people of color, belonging and the lack thereof is the first way that we feel alienated outside of our homes. The workplace, being the place where we, arguably, spend the most time has to rise to imperative levels of importance for purposely creating a sense of belonging. This text, Trust The Process, closely examines the consequences of having a workplace where some, namely the people of color, lack a sense of belonging and how the issue of belonging was successfully addressed. Too many times, we learn about unsuccessful workplace practices and conditions. Here, finally, there is a transferable solution for how to give voice to the voiceless.

Workplace of inclusion

One would think that if a workplace has belonging, then surely it has inclusion, but these two ideas: belonging and inclusion, are not automatically synonymous. For example, in a garden there are earthworms, soil, roots, weeds, thorns, leaves and red roses. Each of these things *belong* in the garden. When the gardener cuts an arrangement for the dinner table only the leaves and the roses are welcomed. The thorns are an unfortunate element that must be dealt with, but the earthworms, soil, roots and weeds, though they all belong in the garden, are not included in the bouquet. People of color in the workplace are too seldom considered roses, and therefor too often not included in the forward making decisions. They aren't part of the bouquet though they belong in the garden (we know that there are exceptions). Inclusion, really, is a social construct based on traditions that must be retaught on purpose, but how? This text gives examples of how reorganization and purposeful inclusion of all the people in the workplace can create a sustainable culture of inclusion.

Workplace of equity

Naturally, without belonging and inclusion there can be no equity. The element that makes equity so difficult for organizations is perception. I believe that perception is where the hardest work is done because the perception is not a view of the workplace, it is a view of the self. Perception is the ask of white allies to examine their privilege and to compassionately consider the experience of living in a world that does not invite or welcome them to be part of the bouquet. For people of color, the whole world is designed for the red roses: the dining room, the table, the runner, the vase were all created with the red rose in mind. Shifted perception and the resulting equity (precursed by belonging and inclusion) allows for the seemingly impossible to become possible. The brave thing about this text is the author's skillful discussion about both white fragility and the quick to draw race card on the part of people of color. This text is a balanced examination that ultimately leads to workplace equity.

Let me say, too, that this writing is a critical and imperative entry into the historical record. It is significant that the place to claim workplace equity achievement includes a group of young attorneys of color which has been the make and model of legal and social progress in the garden that is the United States of America. Surely, Thurgood Marshall, Barbra Jordan, Charles Hamilton Houston and Bryan Stevenson, change makers and bold print asterisks in US legal history, nod at this transformational record and guide on how to make America's workplace equitable.

Talena Lachelle Queen, Poet Laureate, Paterson New Jersey

I

Setting the Context

A. Overview

"Inequality and injustice persist. But they are no match for the human spirit."—Darren Walker, President of Ford Foundation

First let me be clear. This book represents my *own* perspective, experiences and recollections. I am not speaking as a representative of Columbia Legal Services, nor do I suggest that my thoughts represent any particular subset of individuals. In writing this book, I also understand that my experience was unique in that Columbia Legal Services is an organization that is unabashedly and daringly committed to integrating race equity into its organizational culture. I was unlike many of my counterparts who were charged with leading race equity efforts in their organizations, only to discover that their organization's leaders were more committed to "looking like" they were doing the work then actually doing it. This rendered my counterparts ineffective as they struggled to protect and defend their body of work, while at the same time, still being held accountable to deliver results to staff.

This book is intended for leaders who are grappling with ways to transform their organizations into safe, transparent, and equitable spaces where all people are growing and thriving. Because of this, you will read a lot about the leader, but truly this book is really about an entire organization who worked together. This book is also for nonprofits. Nonprofits just have a different culture and more flexibility in how they do this work; and because most have a social justice mission, it is all the more important to me that they understand that how they treat each other is as important as how they treat their clients.

Next, I'll echo the sentiments of esteemed pioneers in this work like Ada Shen-Jaffe, who not only encouraged me to memorialize this journey, but also share it far and wide for those who may want to engage in this work. This is what inspired me most. If there is any way to help an organization or leader save time or frustration by sharing our experience, then I'm all for it. All too often, people tend to be territorial and hold power by denying people access to information - which is part of the racist arrangement that keeps people oppressed. I was also encouraged by our Director, Merf Ehman, who told me for months, "Michelle, you have to write a book about this". Most people who know me know that one of my least favorite things to do is document things. I enjoy strategizing, creating, implementing and facilitating, but documenting what happened, and who said what? So, so painful for me. Writing this book was a way for me to capture the essence of our journey, while hopefully, making a difference for others who are looking to tackle the issue of race equity work in their organizations.

Finally, and this is most important: the title of this book was given to me by two of my favorite CLS friends, Alex and Travis. I think it gets to the heart of this work: Trust. But I'd be remiss if I didn't acknowledge that people of color are all too often asked to "trust" with very little evidence to suggest why they should. In fact, there is more evidence to support that trusting is the exact opposite instinct to have when it comes to racism and trusting white people...*the exact opposite*. For people of color, "Just trust us/me" has resulted in stolen bodies and identities, torture, racial inertia and control, overmedication, under treatment, mass incarceration, the obliteration of communities, groups and tribes, denial of the most basic freedoms of humanity and so, so much more.

So why keep this title? In my opinion, there is NO other way to get to a healthy organization, community, society and world without the elements of trust. Have you ever been in a meeting where someone says, *"I don't feel 'safe'"* to discuss this or share that? All they are saying is "I don't trust you". To continue to hope for any change in a culture where there is no trust makes no sense whatsoever. This is why this book focuses on building relationships upon which trust can be formed. Also, equity work is an ongoing process of falling down, getting up, falling down and getting up again. The key is to keep getting up.

Reflecting on the 45th president's term, it's easy to say that we as a nation had much more work to do than many believed. As our country seemed to become more and more divided on where we stood on issues of justice and equality, Columbia Legal Services (CLS), a small civil legal aid firm in Seattle, was also grappling with its own internal race equity practices and culture. This could be a story about a gutsy bunch of attorneys, paralegals and leaders who were willing to dive into the unknown and tackle the seemingly insurmountable issue of race. This could also be a story of radical leaders that somehow thought it would be a good idea to fight *this* internal battle, *while* working to fight for clients who were suffering from injustice in our state. As the Equity Director charged with leading this effort, this could be my story about a Black woman's journey of leading conversations about race, while grappling with her own insecurities resulting not only from internalized oppression, but simply being *human*.

Quite simply, this is a story about a daring group of people, led by radical leadership, working together to become an anti-racist organization, and all that came along with it. I would even go so far as to say that this is a story about one organization's *healing process*. When working to eradicate racist systems, there comes a time when you have to just 'rip the band-aid off' and allow those organizational wounds to heal in the open air. This can be difficult for some and (re)traumatizing for others. But CLS continues to stay the course of working to heal from racism and racist structures--through mistakes, questions, fears, ups and downs.

CLS is not perfect – not by a long shot. After all, it's a business operated in the male-dominated, eurocentric field of law, and comes with lawyers upon lawyers, I mean, layers upon layers of structural and systemic racism embedded in it.

While I'm no longer working with CLS, I am proud to have been a part of this journey and to bear witness to the struggle and grit of the individuals who engaged... really engaged... in race equity work. Also, so many people who've heard about our work have asked me to speak to, train about, or share the story of CLS and our process to move toward a transparent, restorative and safe organization. Usually, they are seeking tools, tips or strategies to "do the work", which is often code for "check the box"; but, this is not that kind of work.

I've said many times that when we think of social justice work, many organizations and consultants place heavy emphasis on the "justice" aspect. In other words, the systems, structures, and arrangements at play that perpetuate inequality and inequity. While I work with (and love) attorneys, I am a strong believer that changing the 'systems' won't bring about the change we want to see. We are seeing in our nation that it's the "people" in these systems that must change their minds and hearts. This is the "social" aspect of the work. This is the real work of organizational change and healing.

Columbia Legal Services has a strong reputation for its work in fighting for vulnerable communities in Washington state. When it came to our work, I believed in the commitment and passion of every person in our office. Not just the legal staff, but everyone, including our accounting, IT, support, and communications staff. We were pretty clear why we were there. We were on the front lines fighting for people who are (or were) incarcerated, farmworkers, foster care youth, youth in detention, people living under deplorable slumlord conditions, the list goes on. So, in my mind, there was never a doubt that unifying and fighting for *each other* internally would pose any serious challenges.

Oh, but there were challenges.

The main challenge would be for each and every one of us to confront and slay our own personal dragons that racism tends to provoke. We had to move beyond the fear as individuals of looking like or being called racist. We had to learn to give each other space to grapple with the discomfort and not judge one another. We had to learn how to be courageous and speak up for the truth. We had to learn how to be gracious when someone made a mistake. We had to learn how to be an upstander versus a bystander when we see someone being treated unfairly. We had to learn how to embrace discomfort. All. The. Time.

For me, I was most eager for us to learn that this work was not *really* about race, gender identity, ability, tenure or position. I mean it was to some extent, but it really wasn't. This is more about our social connection to one another and ensuring that everyone felt that they mattered. Or even more so, that everyone wanted to *do their part* to ensure that everyone felt they mattered. The question that kept me up at night was, "How do we get people to care about each other in the workplace?" and "Is that even rational?" I believe that when you care about someone, you want them to have the same advantages as you, you are more likely to sort out differences, you are more gracious when they make a mistake, you are more likely to take a risk or be more vulnerable to protect them when you see them being treated unfairly. Also, you are more likely to assume they are just being a jerk as opposed to a racist. Jerks we can live with, but racists?

Indeed, I'll talk about systems and structures, but real sustainable equity, justice, and belongingness cannot be narrowed down to a structure or mechanism. It can't be measured in a year or a president's term. People who approach equity through this framework, will surely meet frustration and fatigue.

I believe that like many other legal/legal aid organizations, our approach to change was historically and instinctively toward legal wins or policy changes, which are both very important. But I also believed that without the core values of empathy, compassion, and fairness *along with* a deep understanding of the inequitable systemic arrangements, these wins would not have as strong of an impact.

This translates to our internal process at CLS. Understanding that true and sustainable equity requires an organizational culture shift of hearts and minds, we decided to take a leap, dig into the work and (at least try to) **trust the process**.

There will likely be leaders of nonprofits who'll read this book and think, "we are bigger than CLS, this would never work here", or "we are smaller than CLS, we don't have the resources", or "we are way too dysfunctional to implement such a comprehensive approach to equity", or "our board isn't diverse (or doesn't value diversity, equity and inclusion principles) and wouldn't support these efforts" etc.

I hear that a lot in my travels, and my goal with sharing CLS's process is to leave universal and bite-sized breadcrumbs that any organization can follow regardless of their size, culture, and resources.

B. In retrospect

CLS Director, Merf Ehman, wrote an article that described her reflections of CLS's race equity journey. I think it offers a clear and comprehensive account from a leader's perspective and I'll therefore share it with you. The following article was written for, and published by the Management Information Exchange (MIE) in the spring 2018 issue, and can be found at www.mielegalaid.org. It is used in this book by permission.

An Examination by Columbia Legal Services Director, Merf Ehman: *Transforming culture - An examination of workplace values through the frame of white dominant culture"*.

culture <u>noun</u> cul·ture \ ˈkəl-chər \

b: <u>the set of shared attitudes</u>, values, goals, and practices that characterizes an institution or organization ("culture").

Every organization has its own culture. It's "the way we do things around here." Some of it is written down and some of it is not. As legal aid organizations consider issues of diversity, race equity, and inclusion we have begun to examine the culture of our organizations.

At Columbia Legal Services we started looking at our culture in depth after we conducted a 2012 diversity survey. That survey found that over 3 in 4 employees witnessed inattention to diversity issues that created negative consequences for staff morale and staff retention. This finding was in spite of an active Inclusion, Diversity and Multiculturalism committee (IDM). We were hiring diverse staff, but not retaining them. We had a statement on IDM issues and conducted regular trainings for staff, but significant issues remained. In the survey, the highest level of satisfaction at our organization was among staff who identified themselves as white, male, and hetero-sexuals. Other groups reported consistently lower satisfaction rates. While satisfaction rates among these groups was discouraging, the level of engagement and attentive critique that staff provided in survey comments revealed a collective desire to grapple with the complex and difficult issue of diversity in the workplace.

As a result of the survey, we revamped our internal volunteer staffed IDM committee and renamed it the Equity Committee and formed several subcommittees, one of which was the Culture Committee. The Culture Committee discussed how to improve staff morale and change the culture at CLS. This committee really struggled to get to the root of the problem and how to address it. We discussed many ways to improve our culture and be more inclusionary - reading a book with a diversity or equity theme together, having more equity trainings, conducting another survey, including IDM issues at staff meetings, figuring out ways to learn more about each other and encouraging staff to exchange ideas and communicate about these issues. We undertook most of these activities. Staff enjoyed them and we learned more about each other and about IDM issues, but after more than two years of implementation we had not experienced a significant change in retention rates of diverse staff. There remained some morale issues as well. We had made forward progress in expanding our range as an organization on IDM issues, however, significant challenges remained.

In other words, we became aware of a problem and acted to fix it. This is exactly one of the problems with what are identified as white cultural norms – "we gave into the pattern of moving from awareness to action without taking the necessary steps that help us to be more effective and successful in reaching our vision and goals." (Dismantling Racism 2016 p. 41). Looking back what we failed to do was to undertake an analysis of our organizational culture, norms, and, power relations. (From White Racist). We did not take time out to reflect on our values as an organization – both explicit and implicit. While we were "good people" trying to make change for the better, we did not consider the dynamics of internal racism, power relations or the need for accountability to people and communities of color. We also did not examine how these issues played out in our advocacy. While we celebrated having a diverse staff and board and had made progress on these issues, we had not yet specifically analyzed our organization through a race equity frame or as an institution working in a legal system that had regularly and systematically reinforced white supremacy. (Dismantling Racism 2016 p. 9-15).

As we undertook this next analysis, we reviewed our office culture through the lens of "white culture." (Racialequitytools.org 2018). (This analysis continues as it is not a static straightforward process). Under this frame, the norms of an organization are examined by looking at dominant cultural norms to see how they play out at work. There are a series of questions that can be asked to help pull one out these underlying assumptions about what is "normal" (Racialequitytools.org 2018). For example, we asked what do we consider the characteristics of a "good" employee? How are people informed about this standard? Are there unwritten rules about this? Is a good employee someone who works long hours or someone who sets good boundaries around work? Is a good employee someone who separates their personal and work life or someone who integrates their life as a whole? Is a good employee someone who does not work when they are sick or someone who tries to work from home or comes in even if ill? Is a good employee someone who comes to work on time or someone who works a flexible schedule? Or both or neither? (Racialequitytools.org 2018).

Our organizations often have values about how people should work and how they should behave without considering how these values were developed. At our organization we continue to think about these questions so that we can be more conscious about what we value and why. This type of evaluation is imperative when trying to make our organizations inclusive because "listing characteristics of white supremacy culture is to point out how organizations which unconsciously use these characteristics as their norms and standards make it difficult, if not impossible, to open the door to other cultural norms and standards." (Dismantling Racism 2016 p. 28) These characteristics are "interconnected and mutually reinforcing –perfectionism, a sense of urgency, defensiveness and/or denial, quantity over quality, worship of the written word, the belief in one right way, paternalism, either/or binary thinking, power hoarding, fear of open conflict, individualism, progress defined as more, the right to profit, objectivity, and the right to comfort." (Okun 2010). These characteristics are particularly valued in the legal profession (Okun 2010 p. 43). Below is a chart about some of the values and behaviors of white culture at work. The chart does not cover all 15 characteristics, but information about them all can be found in the resources in the end notes.

This summary chart is based on the Dismantling Racism 2016 Workbook as well as the information and experiences I had at a recent training - Undoing Racism from People's Institute for Survival and Beyond and mistakes I have made ("Our Principles").

Value	Issues Related to the Value	Antidote (Dismantling Racism 2016 p. 28-35).
Perfectionism (Dismantling Racism 2016 p. 28).	• Point out how the work is inadequate – focus critique on the negative • Talk to others about the inadequacies of a person or their work, but not talk directly to that person • Mistakes are personal – a mistake lowers your value • Little work is put into reflecting on or reviewing lessons learned as a team or organization; rather we move on quickly to the next case or project or send the person to training rather than engaging in a group debriefing • Accolades for winning and success but not for trying and failing • Internal harsh inner critic develops	• Create a culture of appreciation • Become a learning organization where mistakes are the forerunners to new ideas and learning • Create an adaptive culture • See mistakes as learning opportunities rather than an embarrassment • Separate person from the mistake • Support staff to move from internal criticism to sharing mistakes so that others can learn (move self-view from mistake maker to teacher)

Urgency (Dismantling Racism 2016 p. 29).	• Must move quickly so that it becomes impossible to take the time to be inclusive, transparent or thoughtful • Criticism for taking too long to make a decision • Long term thinking is not as valued as being able to "think on your feet" • Sometimes make quick decisions in the legislature or other practice areas that results in sacrificing the interests of communities of color; look for the short term win rather than the longer-term systems change • Reinforced by time limited grants or other funding schemes • Reinforced by the billable hour in six-minute intervals • Being too busy is viewed as being successful • Working long hours or not sleeping to get the work done in time highly valued • Taking time to eat, go to the bathroom or chat with a co-worker viewed as wasting time or suspect	• Engage with staff on developing realistic work plans • Model taking the time to make thoughtful and transparent decisions • Leadership understanding that most things take longer than you expect – this includes writing briefs, collective bargaining, strategic planning, settlements • Include and plan for the time needed to be inclusive in the decision making • Include realistic timeframes in funding proposals • Set clear parameters for how the organization will make decisions when there is an actual crisis and define what constitutes a crisis • Take time to laugh, eat and go to the restroom and connect with co-workers • Support staff to saying no when necessary

Defending (Dismantling Racism 2016 p. 29).	• People respond to new ideas with defensiveness • The organization spends a lot of time trying to make sure that people's feelings are not hurt or working around people who are difficult or defensive • White people spend energy worrying that they might be considered racist instead of examining how racism might actually be happening • People in power make decisions based on whether they can defend the decision	• See defensiveness as a problem and not a solution • Trust your staff; they are more resilient • "Understand the link between defensiveness and fear (of losing power, losing face, losing comfort, losing privilege); work on your own defensiveness" (Dismantling Racism 2016 p. 29). • Develop a set of values together as an organization that are used to make proactive decisions
Writing is the most prized form of communica-tion(Disman-tling Racism 2016 p. 30).	• Writing is considered the highest and best form of communication • staff that struggle with legal writing are considered inferior to those that do not • Strong interpersonal communication skills are considered "soft" skills and less highly valued • There is a specific "right" way to write • Good writing is associated with good thinking (strong analytical skills)	• Value all forms of communication • Understand how storytelling, connecting and visual imagery are essential skills • Value staff that bring diverse forms of communication

| Fear of conflict (Dismantling Racism 2016 p. 33, 35). | • Focus on the person who raised the problem rather than addressing the conflict and the underlying issue.
• Emphasis on being polite
• "Equating the raising of difficult issues with being impolite, rude, or out of line" (Dismantling Racism 2016 p. 33).
• Avoiding conflict | • Allow staff to raise issues without having to do it perfectly
• Understand your own relationship to conflict and encourage others to do so
• Be open that conflict is not an exception; it is part of our working lives
• Consider learning more and embracing principles of restorative justice
• practice and role play with staff "difficult conversations"
• be aware of the assumptions we make when we are having a conflict with someone at work
• "understand that discomfort is at the root of all growth and learning; welcome it as much as you can; deepen your political analysis of racism and oppression so you have a strong understanding of how your personal experience and feelings fit into a larger picture; don't take everything personally" |

Individualism (Dismantling Racism 2016 p. 33).	• Staff are asked to work in teams, but do so in name only • Discomfort working as a team • "Accountability, if any, goes up and down, not sideways to peers or to those the organization is set up to serve" • Focus on individual successes and achievements • Creates feelings of isolation • Feeling in offices that there is not a team, but rather several solo practitioners sharing space • Little time or resources devoted to developing skills in how to cooperate or work collaboratively • "Creates a lack of accountability, as the organization values those who can get things done on their own without needing supervision or guidance"	• Provide training and support for collaborative work and thinking i.e. teach people how to work in teams • Include teamwork in our values • Explain and make explicit the ways teamwork improves outcomes • "Evaluate people's ability to work in a team as well as their ability to get the job done" • Support a culture where it is the norm to bring an issue to the group rather than have it be solved by an individual • Create an atmosphere where all meetings (staff, intake, case review, project or team meetings) are used to solve problems rather than just report information
Objectivity (Dismantling Racism 2016 p. 34).	• Assuming policies are neutral and objective without conducting an analysis of possible racial implications • Seeing emotions as removed from the decision-making processes • Prioritizing or requiring linear and logical thinking over other types of thinking or imagining	• Appreciate everyone's way of seeing and thinking about the world and how that impacts the way their understanding of the world • Understand that discomfort with different approaches or ways of thinking can be a positive experience • Listen • Start with the assumption that everyone has a valid point • Try to understand that point.

Understanding this framework is essential:

[O]rganizations which unconsciously use these characteristics as their norms and standards make it difficult, if not impossible, to open the door to other cultural norms and standards. As a result, many of our organizations, while saying we want to be multicultural, really only allow other people and cultures to come in if they adapt or conform to already existing cultural norms. Being able to identify and name the cultural norms and standards you want is a first step to making room for a truly multicultural organization (Dismantling Racism 2016 p. 35).

We started this process by creating caucus teams that included The Collective (made of persons of color in the organization) and a white allies group. Participation in either team is voluntary. The Collective sent a letter to all staff pointing out the ongoing problematic issues in our organization and calling for us to become #OneCLS. This letter was painful for some white staff to read and process; others were excited that this conversation was happening and some attributed it to "whining."

Within this letter, The Collective suggested solutions. Management implemented the suggestions that it could implement right away and the rest were addressed through a two-month staff-wide process where management stepped aside except to provide support and information as needed. Staff formed teams to address each issue area and draft suggested policy or process changes. We held our first annual Equity Day in 2017 where staff presented their proposals to everyone. Following this work, we set out to implement the policies (policies available on request). Everyone in the organization had a chance to comment on them. Part of this work also included starting the process of adopting restorative justice values into the internal work of our organization. We also all worked together at our subsequent staff retreat to adapt values for how we interact with each other #OneCLS. These include:

1. We choose to be conscious of our differences and the uniqueness of others
2. We choose to be accountable for our impact
3. We choose to listen with kindness and compassion
4. We choose to communicate with respect
5. We seek to understand before rushing to judgment

We try to see this process as an unfolding and ongoing journey that we are taking together as an organization. We are moving toward becoming a transformative and anti-racist organization (People's Institute p. 31-33). We are not there yet, but this is our vision:

Based on an analysis of the history of racism and power in this country, this organization supports the development of anti-racist white allies and empowered people of color through the organization's culture, norms, policies and procedures.

The Anti-Racist Organization integrates this commitment into the program, helping white people work together and challenge each other around issues of racism, share power with people of color, take leadership from and be accountable to people of color, feel comfortable with being uncomfortable while understanding that we are all learning all the time.

The Anti-Racist Organization helps people of color become more empowered through taking leadership, sharing of power, transforming the organizational norms and culture, challenging white allies and other people of color, sharing in decisions about how the organizations' resources will be spent, what work gets done as well as how it gets done, the setting of priorities, and allowing people of color to make the same mistakes as white people. The organization does this by forming caucuses for both white and people of color, providing training and encouraging discussions about racism, white privilege, power, accountability, setting clear standards for inclusion at all levels of the organization, reviewing the mission, vision, policies, procedures, board agreements, etc. to ensure that the commitment to end racism is a consistent theme, helping people to understand the links between the oppressions, and devoting organizational time and resources to building relationships across race and other barriers.[xxvi]

We are excited about this work going forward. Our internal transformation process will impact how we undertake advocacy and what we focus on. We hope to instill these principles in all of our work. This process has not been linear or comfortable. We have looked to other organizations who are leading in this area. We in legal aid are in the process of changing our cultural values from those steeped in white law firm culture to those rooted in transformation and anti-racist work. Ours is but one story among many other legal aid organizations taking on this work. We look forward to hearing your stories.

"Culture." *Merriam-Webster*, 2018, Merriam-Webster, www.merriam-webster.com/dictionary/culture

Dismantling Racism 2016 Workbook, *dR Works, p. 41*. https://resourcegeneration.org/wp-content/uploads/2018/01/2016-dRworks-workbook.pdf

Dismantling Racism 2016 Workbook, p. 9-15; Race – The Power of an Illusion, Film Transcript for Episode 3 (sets out the ways policies and subsequent related court decisions advantaged certain groups over others) http://www.pbs.org/race/000_About/002_04-about-03-01.htm; History of Racism and Immigration Time Line, Racial Equity Tools (stops at 2005) http://www.racialequitytools.org/resource-files/racismimmigration-timeline.pdf; A History of Racial Injustice, Equal Justice Initiative (through 2010) https://racial-injustice.eji.org/timeline/2010s/; http://www.eraseracismny.org/structural-racism-timeline.

From White Racist to White Anti-Racist, Tema Okun, dR Works https://wwhatsup.files.wordpress.com/2014/10/wwhatsup-week3-readings1.pdf/

Racialequitytools.org. (2018). [online] Available at: http://www.racialequitytools.org/images/uploads/N._White_Culture_Handout.pdf [Accessed 17 Oct. 2018].

Okun, Tema. *The emperor has no clothes: Teaching about race and racism to people who don't want to know.* IAP, 2010.

"Our Principles." *The People's Institute for Survival and Beyond*, www.pisab.org/our-principles.

People's Institute Handout, Continuum on Becoming an Anti-Racist Multicultural Institution at p. 31-33.

end

C. You, the Leader

Organizational anti-racism work carries with it a considerable amount of pressure on the leader to hold a vision that seems almost irrational at times. It requires that leaders learn how to balance the ability to hold a strong belief for change, while dealing with the day-to-day realities of living in a racist country, and overcoming historical organizational inequities that many people in the organization may still be healing from. So let the games begin!

The Bridgespan Group is a global nonprofit organization that consults with organizations to help them strengthen their organizational capacity, develop leaders, and align their social justice principles with their operating practices.

When it comes to building a race equity culture within organizations, Bridgespan's report *Awake to Woke to Work: Building a Race Equity Culture* suggests that all organizations undergo the following three stages which they have coined, 'The Race Equity Cycle':

- **Awake:** Increased *representation* in organizations, focused on increasing the number of people of different race backgrounds
- **Woke:** Greater *inclusion*, aimed at internal change in behaviors, policies, and practices so that everyone is comfortable sharing their experiences and is equipped to talk about race inequities
- **Work:** Consistent *application* of a race equity lens to examine how organizations and programs operate

While I wholeheartedly agree with the phases, I don't necessarily agree with the order. Reflecting back on our process, I'd suggest flipping-steps one and two as follows:

1. **Awake:** Greater inclusion of existing staff, focusing on a change in behavior, policies, practices, and greater ease of sharing of experiences. One thing I've observed is the **crucial mistake** of hiring more diverse staff without first changing the culture that they are hired into. In my experience, this only adds to the problem.
2. **Woke:** Once the culture of the organization has started to shift, and there is a critical mass of staff who are on board with the vision, then bringing in new staff seems to make more sense. In this way, you are building and strengthening your organizational culture with people who are aligned to the new vision.

I would say that no matter how small or large your organization is, you should focus on the existing staff by making sure they understand your vision and commitment to becoming an anti-racist organization. Your existing staff will be your greatest allies or your biggest obstacles.

So, let's go back to the beginning. In October 2015, CLS underwent a white fragility training led by Robin DiAngelo. Like most of Robin's trainings, it was *intense* to say the least. There were tears shed, people stormed out of the room and it was painfully clear that CLS had A LOT of work to do regarding issues of race and racism. Our then Executive Director, Aurora Martin, realized that we as an organization had reached a critical point where we could no longer ignore the internal divide between staff of color and white staff. She took immediate action to address what could be considered an organizational crisis.

The first step she took was making the **commitment** to address race in a real, meaningful and sustainable way. All too often, the idea of beginning a race equity movement is born out of a reaction to a conflict, or grievance or maybe even a lawsuit. This perspective sets the wrong context because once the conflict is over, or the grievance is settled, so is the urgency of equity work. The most beneficial way to approach this work is to view it as a PROACTIVE response to organizational transformation as opposed to a REACTIVE response to a problem.

The second step she took was to **invest** in an internal position that would oversee the process to ensure that race equity work continued and didn't become another failed attempt at "doing the work". I appreciated the fact that she resisted the urge to bring in a *hired gun* consultant, but instead looked at this work as an ongoing part of our work. She did consider an external hire, but realized that this would be best led by "one of our own". She appointed me, the Development Director at the time, to lead the charge. My role was soon changed to Equity Director and, as the saying goes, the rest is history.

I often get the question of whether or not to bring in an external consultant or appoint an internal staff member to run point on initiatives as potentially combustible as race equity. If you are going to select an internal candidate, I would suggest doing what Aurora did. She appointed an internal full-time staff member to lead the work of #OneCLS. I believe this was both a symbolic and practical decision. Symbolically, she was sending a clear message that she took equity seriously. What we know about most nonprofits are that their resources are limited. We also know that organizations, nonprofits and otherwise, put their resources where their values are. By allocating resources to this position, she was making a considerable commitment to this work and establishing race equity as an organizational value. Practically, this work just couldn't be done by allocating a portion of an FTE. For example, if an attorney would have taken on this role, I am quite certain that once their caseload became overloaded, the equity work would have taken a back seat. This applies to anyone else who had another primary role. In these cases, equity becomes more of a "project" rather than an initiative worthy of the focus it demands. Also, there was a lot of work to be done, and even for a full-time position, at times it felt overwhelming.

If you choose to hire an external consultant, they would need to have the time and bandwidth to build relationships with staff, which can be tough. In my experience, consultants symbolize an "in and out" model of change. "I'll tell you what to do and you do it." Thoroughly integrating equity work requires daily attention and focus. It demands space for people to process in an official and unofficial capacity. It demands a person who is familiar with the pulse of the organization to make decisions to proceed with an idea, halt a particular process or make instinctual calls. Many of these demands are hard to meet with a consultant. If you can't hire from within, conduct an external search for someone to join staff as a dedicated leader in your race equity efforts. It is my opinion that hiring a consultant should be the last option.

If you do hire a consultant, remember we are talking about race. This is not "technical" work. This will need to be someone who is well trained in conversations and matters of race, equity and *humanity*. They will need to have a higher social emotional intelligence as people often misfire their frustrations at the person whom they perceive to be making them deal with their discomfort.

The third thing Aurora did was allocate organizational resources toward officializing The Collective and the white allies group to give space for groups to share experiences and unpack racism within their own racial identity groups. I can't speak highly enough of the value of creating spaces for structured, intentional, healthy conversations of race within your own identity groups. We'll discuss this more in an upcoming chapter.

Lastly, Aurora mandated our first Equity Day where we gathered as an organization with the sole purpose to discuss race within our organization. This was not easy. In fact, it was termed "e-quit" day as people anticipated the discomfort of driving one hour into the woods and talking about race for an entire day. Again, more on Equity Day to come in a later chapter.

While Aurora's tenure would soon be over, she ushered in a new era in CLS's history that our new director would then expand upon.

A new leadership chapter

Several months later, Merf Ehman was promoted from Staff Attorney to Executive Director. I was particularly excited because Merf had been actively engaged in racial justice work and I knew that Aurora's vision would continue in innovative and expansive ways.

I have had conversations with the leadership of several nonprofit organizations who ask about "the work" of institutionalizing race equity. Eventually the conversation ends with a discussion about *the leader* it takes to do this work. I can't speak for all organizations, but I can share some of the characteristics I observed that I found to be extremely powerful (and refreshing) when doing this work.

1. Clear Why

Author and motivational speaker Simon Sinek says that everyone has a "why". In his well-known Ted Talk, "*Start with Why*", he states that every person knows *what* they do, some of us know *how* we do it, but very few are clear about *why* we do what we do. He further believes that those who are clear about their why, are the ones who are able to weather the storms they face in business and eventually become successful.

I would argue that everyone at CLS knew our why when it came to serving our clients. But when it came to the work of #OneCLS, it was easy to lose sight, especially in times of upheaval. However, Merf was good at galvanizing us by bringing us back to our why. At the top of Merf's "why" playlist I heard a few predominant themes. First, she believed that creating conditions of safety, transparency and equity would foster an environment where people grew and enjoyed being at CLS. When we were voting on our values as the leadership team, one of her values that she put up a strong fight for was "playfulness". She understood our work is hard enough and enjoying what we do would give us the wherewithal to stay motivated and encouraged. Second, she believed that dealing with our hidden biases would only make us better equipped to serve our clients who come from all types of backgrounds, experiences and belief systems. Third, as Merf stated in her interview, she holds a strong value for fairness and doing what's right.

When things got difficult, we always had a *'why'* to bring us back into alignment. As a leader do you know your why? What is your motivation for doing this work?

2. Vulnerability

What I've learned is that vulnerability is not a weakness. In fact, vulnerability requires tremendous strength and courage. Not being understood, accepted or liked is a concern for many people, especially for leaders. A leader can only be vulnerable to the extent that they can accept themselves – even those things they don't necessarily like or are ashamed of.

    a.   **Taking off the armor** - Not surprisingly, organizational leaders take the hit for everything that goes wrong. Depending on the organizational culture this can have a debilitating effect on leaders if they are not clear, grounded and confident. After a while, many leaders choose to create mechanisms to protect themselves. These mechanisms can range from blaming others, being unwilling to make firm decisions and stick to them, to not connecting with staff on a personal level.

Vulnerable leaders will *lean in* to the discomfort. One thing that we did was have a check-in at the beginning of each meeting. Merf was particularly honest about where she was in the moment. "I'm irritated/cranky", "I'm overwhelmed". Also, she would sometimes get triggered by a conversation and admit, "I'm triggered right now. I'm pretty sensitive about this subject matter, or that thing. I know I need to work on that". Because of this, we were able to understand that her reaction wasn't personal which helped keep the lines of communication open. It also created an atmosphere where we could be honest about how we felt in the moment.

b. **Being okay with not knowing.** Many leaders are often expected to have all the answers. I have been in leadership roles in which I felt embarrassed, or avoided situations because I didn't have the answer. Both Aurora and Merf were really good at stepping back and saying, "I don't know. Let me think about it." Merf was especially good at saying "I'm curious to know what you think?" allowing me to be a meaningful thought partner in our decisions. I always felt that Merf trusted my judgment and more times than not gave me the room and resources to try different ideas.

3. Radical Transparency

Ray Dalio, founder and CEO of Bridgewater, the world's largest hedge fund, says he runs his company on the principle of radical transparency. He said, *"My most important principle is that getting at the truth, whatever it may be, is essential for getting better. We get at truth through radical transparency and putting aside our ego barriers in order to explore our mistakes and personal weaknesses so that we can improve."*

When I've had conversations about radical transparency, most leaders hear, "giving up control". This is understandable because information is power, and giving people access to information feels like relinquishing control. However, what I've observed is that for real change to occur, people need to have the experience of choice. People can only choose what they understand, which is where transparency comes in.

I'll never forget one of CLSs former Directors, Ada Shen-Jaffe, who told our leadership team, "During times of change, major decision-making, or organizational stress, you need to increase your communication by a factor of ten". She was speaking of radical transparency. We had to consistently deliver communication that was clear, current and specific so that people understood how and why we were making decisions – eventually (however slowly) gaining trust and improving psychological safety with staff.

In addition to transparency was the challenge to be *consistent*. I appreciated that Merf's position and message about her vision for CLS never wavered. Not only did I perceive her actions to be consistent with her message, but her *reasoning behind the actions* tied back to that message. Even if adhering to a new process or new plan took longer or more effort, it was more important to stay true to our message as a leadership body than compromise the trust of staff. For example, there were times when we needed to make some quick decisions and it sure would have been easier to make a unilateral decision and keep it pushing. But because of our commitment to transparency, we had to communicate to all staff what we had decided, the process that we went through to come to that decision and, in some cases, give people a window of time to weigh in on it. This slowed our process down considerably. But that was the cost that Merf was willing to pay. No doubt, I can say that Merf made some missteps, and there were misunderstandings or miscommunications along the way, but for the most part, she was clear and stayed consistent.

Many people struggle with equity work because it requires an honest reflection that demands people to own some unpopular (or even ugly) truths about themselves. Also, they don't want to look bad or even worse, racist. With a strong leader who embraces conflict, makes and owns mistakes, and demonstrates vulnerability, this work is considerably easier. Reading ahead, you'll see how these traits will prove to be beneficial.

As for some actionable steps you can take as a leader, Bridgespan's report, *Awake to Woke to Work: Building a Race Equity Culture*, offers the following as a starting point on building a race equity culture.

1. **Establish a shared vocabulary.** Create a common language around race equity work.

One thing that I can say for sure is that when it comes to race, race equity, and race equity *in the workplace*, people have very different understandings of what to talk about and how to talk about it. As the leader, this isn't something that you want to leave to individual interpretation. You'll want to make sure that everyone shares a common language. Using the glossary contained in the aforementioned report by Bridgespan may prove to be helpful.

2. **Identify race equity champions at the board and senior leadership levels.**

For every movement, there are the early adopters who get on board and evangelize the work. These are the folks who you'll want to identify and lock arms with. In addition to board members or leadership, don't forget staff members who may not hold positional authority, but most certainly hold power of influence. Also, don't make the mistake of being so hyper-focused on the negative individuals that you miss the opportunity to draw organizational strength from those who are aligned with your vision.

3. **Name race equity work as a strategic imperative.**

Demonstrate how it connects to the organization's mission, vision, organizational values, and strategies.

I'd add to this step to be transparent about race equity work as a moral imperative – especially as it relates to serving clients. Nonprofits generally serve client populations that suffer from poverty, oppression and marginalization and who are very often people of color. While this can be a strategic imperative that ties to your organizational mission and values, it's also a call to humanity that we all be aware of how systems and structures affect people who are not white. This starts within the four walls of the organization.

4. Open a continuous dialogue about race equity work.

When CLS began the process of race equity movement that continues to this day, I can say that the early days of talking about race were brutal. It took months and months of trainings, caucusing, messages from leadership and other forms of formal and informal conversations to begin the process of slowly breaking down some of the barriers where authentic dialogue could be had. To curate opportunities for deeper conversations about race and race equity in your organization, I've added some resources at the back of this book.

5. Disaggregate data.

People really love hard data to validate their investments, claims, or hard work. But it's also a great tool to reveal quantifiable inequities such as pay gaps, success gaps, and satisfaction gaps within the organization. For the fundraising folks out there, you know how much funders love data. For me, the real motivation is for organizations to be honest about their areas of strength as well as weakness so that they can transform them. Or said another way, you can't heal what you won't reveal.

I believe that an organization's leader is the x-factor in ensuring the transformation of the organizational culture toward racial justice, or reinforcing existing systems of inequity and exclusion. Leading a movement such as race equity requires continued self-examination and reflection; as well as a willingness to make mistakes, be vulnerable enough to own them, and stay faithful to the vision.

4. For People of Color Leading an Equity Movement - On the Front Lines

I can't speak to the experience of leading an organization's equity work as a white person. One, because I don't know a white person who is successfully leading this work *inter*-organizationally, and two, because I'm not white. I do know some powerful white facilitators and consultants, but leading the work from *within* is considerably different from leading this work as a consultant. That said, I am addressing this section specifically to people of color who are leading their organization's race equity initiatives.

I have had the opportunity to learn a lot while doing this work, and there is still so much to learn. The most important thing for me was to figure out a way to stay grounded as a woman of color leading this effort. I sought out other women of color who were doing this work and eventually found a community of people who I could lean on for encouragement, resources, ideas, and strength. In so doing, I was able to become more comfortable in the discomfort and give more of myself without losing myself.

I was also able to learn that many of the things I was experiencing were quite normal. Normalizing breakdowns, roadblocks and challenges helped me approach them with more calm deliberation, focus and peace.

This work can be taxing and is absolutely NOT for the faint at heart. Many people who do this work, soon hit a wall of exhaustion, feeling overwhelmed or frustrated. Again, this is where having a supportive network comes in. My colleagues and I shared many stories over the last two years that revealed some of the different factors that can be at play as you do this work.

***You* are human.** You are surviving *in* a racist framework while simultaneously trying to lead people *beyond* it. This requires being hopeful when there is despair, frustration, and pain all around you. I can recall an instance during one of the more recent trials when yet another police officer was found not guilty of murdering an unarmed Black man. I was led to a near breaking point in doing this work. I tried to push through that day, but it only got worse for every minute that I stayed at work. I remember the awkward silence and discomfort of my leadership team when I went into the ugly cry in a meeting. I mean, who knows what to say, *or keep saying*, every time this happens? My colleagues would try to console or support me, which only made me feel worse having to now manage *their* helplessness as they tried to find the right thing to do or say. I think it's important to make room for our own vulnerabilities, tender spots and triggers - as well as our strengths. It made all the difference in the world; having a circle of support to unpack my feelings, and take care of myself.

Your leader is human. So your leader is engaged, committed and walking the walk. Then, one day their buttons are pushed and you see a side of them that calls into question their real attitudes and beliefs about race, and/or power. You may witness their disagreeable behavior, or you may be the target of it. Either way, you, as the person leading this equity work must speak up, and address the behavior, especially if it was public. The last thing you want is the staff to lose trust in the leader behind their lapse in judgment. I know it's hard to "call someone out", especially if you respect and like them, but not only do you want send a message that the behavior is not ok, but it's also an opportunity to help the leader grow and deal with some of their hidden beliefs that may still lurk deep beneath the surface. If you do not have a relationship with your leader that allows you to have a honest conversation with them, then find and recommend a coach who can. Of course some leaders are simply unwilling to confront and acknowledge their behavior, in which case, you'll have to make some decisions about how to proceed with the work. See below section, "Know when to jump ship". The key here is to know the *spirit* and *intention* of your leaders actions. Some mistakes are slight and misguided, and others are deep cutting and nasty. Most often, we can tell the difference.

Your leadership team just may not be aligned. Doing this work can reveal some deeper issues in leadership teams. In the beginning, I was clear that some people on our leadership team saw my body of work as peripheral. This led them to relate to it, *and me*, as "just one more thing on their plate". This some times made my work very Sisyphus-esque. It was troubling, but what I knew was that Merf had a bigger vision that she was implicitly and explicitly wedded to so I felt it was only a matter of time before our leadership team was in lock step with this work. This gave me hope during the times when I felt that we weren't aligned. If your leader is committed to the work but other members of leadership aren't, then there is a huge opportunity to collaborate with your leader to bring others along.

Your leader may not be aligned. Sometimes it's the leadership team that is committed to the work and the leader isn't, or the leader is more concerned about funders, the board etc. In these cases, you as a team will need to first get clear about the strength of your collective power, and come up with a plan to engage your leader. Your approach will be different for every leader. For example, if you have a data-driven leader, you may need to put together a detailed 12-month execution plan of how you will approach this work including milestones, time-lines, outcomes and objectives, and who will be responsible for each task.

Know when to jump ship. Some of my colleagues have shared stories of tokenism or the experience of being assigned to make changes without having a real voice. For our roles as leaders in race efforts to be successful, the leader must be clear and willing to "call in" others on the leadership team who are not aligned to the greater vision. If your leader/leadership team doesn't have your back, there is no way I'd advise people to stay in this role, unless, the leadership team is strong and cohesive enough to unify and bring in the leader. Or unless your leader is so strongly committed to the vision that they are willing to deal rigorously with anyone on the leadership team who isn't. Many of the people who do this work successfully are usually strong-willed and persistent. But what comes along with this is the urge to dig deeper when things get more and more toxic as opposed to walking away. If you are one of those folks who knows you have issues with walking away from toxic situations, this is for you. Here's a hint. If you often find yourself in situations where you are saying, "I can't leave until I know that I've done everything I can do", then perhaps you should take some extra time to reflect on this role (and your ego) and whether or not you should continue this fight or jump ship.

Don't take it personally. I experienced people behaving in manipulative and deceitful ways. While race may be the cover story, beneath the surface there are people with unresolved issues from childhood, loveless relationships or other miserable conditions at home, insecurities, mental well-being issues that they are desperately trying to manage, physical health conditions, financial concerns, this list goes on. So, sometimes tapping on the race "nerve" will activate any number of these issues. Keeping this in mind has helped me find a sense of compassion when dealing with people in this work. Now, there are people who really do suffer from superiority complex and buy into the "white people are better" narrative. None of this has anything to do with you so try to resist the urge to reform, or change anyone's beliefs. They will resist, challenge you/your logic and in some cases sabotage your efforts. Still...not personal. What helped me most in this process was to stay on message – whatever your message is. I consistently said to everyone, "There's no rulebook here and we should acknowledge ourselves for doing this work the best we can", or "I don't have all the answers so let me hear yours". I never (or at least tried not to) make myself the authority who had all the answers. I'd run for the hills if someone approached me with a *"Seven step guide to transforming into an anti-racist organization"* manual. That's ridiculous. Plus, when you position yourself as the "know it all" person, people will want to discredit the race equity work, by discrediting you. But it's harder to discredit people who are already saying they don't have all the answers and seeking collaborative input.

On more than one occasion I wished I'd been better about documenting. While there are many reasons while people behave inappropriately or destructively, no one should put up with mistreatment from anyone and if it comes down to it, documenting is the best protection we have to protect ourselves against individuals who are sabotaging our efforts.

More times than not, my experience is that people generally want things to get better, but the issue is more about people's threshold for discomfort and how deeply they are willing to interrogate their own perspectives. I'll talk more about that in the next section. Also, realize that people will associate YOU with their discomfort in discussing race, and sometimes lash out. #partofthegig

Humans are designed to survive. Period. I remember when I was talking to my doctor about my sleep apnea. He said that my sleep study concluded that depending on the position I was sleeping in, I would stop breathing up to 16 times per hour. He said that I was so tired because "the body, in its infinite wisdom to stay alive, actually stops letting you go into deep REM sleep. It says, 'uh oh, we need to make sure that she keeps breathing by any means necessary, so we'll make sure she doesn't go into deep sleep since she stops breathing'". So, of course, I asked, "what should I do?" He said the easiest way was to lose 30 pounds and recommended we start there. My next question was, "Is there anything *else* I can do?"

My body was trying to survive apnea by not letting me go into deep sleep. Many people try to survive racism by not going into deep truth - it's just too much work. As much as I desperately needed sleep, I was more concerned about what I'd have to *give up* to get that good sleep. Saying no to certain foods, getting up at ridiculous times to work out, meal prepping? No thank you. I'd rather just drink more water, sleep on one side, go to bed earlier and hope for the best. Similarly, for many white people, eradicating racism is juxtaposed to "giving something up". Giving up comfort, privilege, power, money, etc. It's just easier to think "I'll just meditate on world peace, go to implicit bias trainings, do yoga, eat organic, drive a Prius, vote for Obama and hope for the best." We humans will do just about anything to make ourselves feel like we are dealing with something that we aren't dealing with.

So, people's resistance to your work is about them surviving their realities, instead of dealing with the discomfort of changing it.

Also, some people's entire lives have been about racism and how "the other", whoever that may be, is inferior, less than, unworthy, etc. So to change their position after so long would force them to completely confront their entire life. Again, it's easier to stay the course. In some cases, they will even provoke you to the point where you'll want to react in a negative manner. This serves only to justify their assessment of you or another person of color, or woman... whoever 'the other' is.

Be discerning - Look out for issues of race, but know it's not always about race. I had a colleague share a story about investigating a race claim between a white manager (we'll call him Dan) and his black colleague that reported to him (we'll call her Sharon). For whatever reason, Dan had been short, curt and sometimes rude with Sharon. In meetings, he would cut her off and often left her out of communications that she needed to be able to do her job. Sharon claimed that Dan faintly called her a bitch under his breath one day, but it was so low she couldn't prove it. The final blow was not offering Sharon a promotion that everyone knew she undeniably deserved. As my colleague investigated further, she noticed that Dan treated other women of color (including other Black women) with kindness, respect and was more than willing to support them as they needed. It was night and day. Nothing made sense until one day a young lady came to visit Dan. This young lady was his daughter. She approached

Sharon and exclaimed, "Whoa! You look just like my mom". The young woman was so struck by the resemblance she whipped out her phone and showed a picture of a woman who looked so much like Sharon, that even Sharon, herself was startled by it. Come to find out, there had been a bitter, heartbreaking divorce that Dan was still grieving about. No one mentioned his 60+ pound weight gain, increased absences, decrease in work quality etc. During the investigation, another coworker mentioned that he had made a casual statement about ending his life, but they blew it off. This investigation was purely a race-based claim in the beginning, but then turned into Family and Medical Leave Act (FMLA) leave. He took some time off and came back three months later, healthier and in a better place. He actually ended up recommending the colleague for a promotion that was higher than the one he denied her for.

Because racism is so prevalent, it is instinctive to make assumptions about a particular instance being race-based or racialized. I think it's important for those of us engaged in this work to do our due diligence to demonstrate that we are measured, balanced and thoughtful in how we approach our work.

Finally, if you see something, say something. One struggle I had was calling things out. I wanted to avoid the disruption or discomfort of calling someone out, *whether white or a person of color*, about things that were counteractive to our movement. This is important to do because it establishes you as a person committed to the vision, above all else.

Organizational readiness. Even if your leader is ready to do this work, the organization (i.e. culture, timing, climate, etc.) may not be ripe for it. It's important to know the difference between excitement and readiness for this work especially when you are the person on the frontline responsible for it. There are many tools out there such as the tool offered at www.racialequitytools.org. They have a pretty comprehensive assessment tool that will help you gauge your organization's capacity for this work. This work isn't about executing the perfect plan or getting it "right". This is 100% a human process of growth, patience and relationship building. It will get messy, clunky and you'll likely want to throw in the towel. If you haven't at least wanted to smack yourself for jumping into this, you're probably not making much of a difference. Expect conflicts and challenges. If you are a perfectionist and are wedded to this vision of the "right" outcome, you will be absolutely miserable and will most likely fail or drive others to become miserable.

This work is tough but necessary and I applaud those of you who have been willing to jump in and consistently expand your range and capacity to better serve your organizations.

D. The Collective Letter

Following the October 2015 white fragility training, it was clear that we needed to prioritize race equity work for staff of color to feel safe, supported, and valued for their contributions. Immediately following the training, 18 staff of color formed the group "The Collective", whose mission was to have a place for staff of color to come together, share experiences and strategically support CLS in being a place that was equitable, collegial, transparent, enjoyable, productive, and safe for all employees.

In May 2016, The Collective sent a letter to all staff highlighting the historical and current racial climate within CLS, with the ultimate goal of creating awareness and urgency of the issues that needed to be addressed related to race. The letter below, now known as **"The Collective Letter"**, was the genesis of an organizational movement that proclaimed that "we are **one** team and will not be divided or treat each other differently based on our racial differences". **The movement is called #OneCLS.**

I had a conversation with every member of The Collective to ask for their permission to share this letter in this book. I was expecting a lot of mixed reactions to this idea of *"airing our dirty laundry"*. But the reaction was the complete opposite. There were cheers and congratulatory support for both the book and the letter being in it. The best statement I heard was, "Go for it Michelle, I look forward to reading more Collective Letters coming out in other organizations." I still remain moved by their support, generosity and love.

That said, after some reflection, I decided to exclude some of the more raw portions of the letter, while still keeping the essence of the letter intact. This letter took 18 people three months to write and in honor of those 18 people, I thought it was important to preserve and respect their most intimate thoughts, feelings, and experiences by not sharing them to a general audience. Secondly, the nature of the information shared by The Collective could leave a perception about CLS that is not intended. Like many organizations, CLS had, and still has its challenges. This book is intended to highlight the tremendous effort, time, and dedication of the staff and leadership to move beyond its past and create a new future.

To be clear, I have not added or paraphrased any content. I have however, excluded several pages' worth of content.

My commitment is that you, the reader, read the following letter and walk away with a formula or format to draft such a document in your own organization. But, even more importantly, my hope is that you are able to feel the grace, commitment and thoughtfulness of the words therein.

Memorandum

To: Columbia Legal Services

From: Collective CLS

Date: May 11, 2016

Re: The Collective CLS Vision Statement: Establishing Racial Equity at CLS

"If you want to go fast, go alone. If you want to go far, go together."-African Proverb

Thank you for the opportunity to address issues of racial equity (Racialequitytools.org 2018) within Columbia Legal Services (CLS). The core mission of CLS is to advocate for people living in poverty (Racialequitytools.org 2018). CLS is an organization that since its inception has been committed to fighting for justice for low income people. When examining poverty in the United States, race is one of the biggest indicators of whether a person must face the harsh realities of economic inequality. Race and poverty are so intertwined that CLS must look at both in order to address racial equity within the program and its advocacy. CLS should not only advocate for its clients to be treated equitably, it should also advocate for its employees to be treated equitably within the program.

During our 2015 All Staff Retreat, we discussed some of the racial challenges we face as an organization. It is exciting to see our Executive Director and our colleagues' commitment to this very important issue. We understand that dealing with matters of race can be uncomfortable and sometimes difficult, but if CLS is committed to ensuring that our culture and advocacy reflects principles of equity, it must face the sobering reality that some staff experience the same marginalization as the clients we work so hard to protect and serve.

The Collective Vision: ONE CLS.

Our perception is that there are many different experiences of CLS. We contend that there should be ONE CLS where one's experience is not heavily influenced by one's position, length of time, and arguably one's race. An intern, legal assistant, paralegal, attorney, accountant, or any staff of color should have the same experience, opportunities and respect. The Collective envisions an organization (based on the Racial Equity Resource Guide's definition of racial equity) in which one's race in no way factors into how they are perceived, the opportunities they are afforded and the investment that is made into their professional and leadership development(Racialequitytools.org 2018). We hope that you read and truly **hear** our message, in its spirit of honesty, with a goal of collaboration and respect, as we work to address the issues and move toward ONE CLS.

Who is Collective CLS and what is its position on racial equity?

Collective CLS ("The Collective") is comprised of 18 CLS staff of color (representing 34% of total staff) that have come together to highlight the historical and current racial climate and concerns within CLS with the ultimate goal of establishing an equitable, safe, and transparent organization for *all* employees (Racialequitytools.org 2018). To reach this goal, we believe it is necessary to understand and contend with the racial, cultural, and structural factors that can prohibit this reality for staff of color.

The Collective's intent is not to call out staff or CLS as racist, because, "when you use the term 'racism,' people are inclined to see a specific person – a racist. However, a racist is not necessary to produce structural outcomes. Instead, institutional interactions generate racialized outcomes." (Poverty and Race 2013). The Collective notes that there are practices, cultural norms, and institutional arrangements that create and maintain disparate racialized outcomes within CLS; many are not intended.

We also believe that management, leadership, and our colleagues can work together towards authentic, sustainable solutions that promote ONE CLS as an equitable, collegial, enjoyable, productive, and safe place to work for all employees committed to successfully advocating for people who face injustice and poverty.

To succinctly articulate the areas of concern, this letter is organized into three sections: 1) identification of issues that impact staff of color, 2) proposed solutions recommended by The Collective, and 3) Conclusion.

I. Identification of Issues that Impact Staff of Color

The Collective acknowledges the thoughtful steps CLS has made to address some of the concerns we mention in this memo. However, as we move toward ONE CLS, it is important to note that there are still individuals who do not hold the same value for race equity as others. Until there is institutional reflection, buy-in and enforcement of race equity in our organization, race equity will remain *a good idea* held by a few, but never actualized. Based on our shared experiences, discussions, and observations, staff of color have identified four areas that highlight our collective experience and perception of marginalization. They are: 1) Office Culture, 2) Leadership Development, 3) The Hiring Process, and 4) Problem Solving of Employee Concerns.

To create both a concrete and abstract understanding of our concerns in these four areas, we have broken each area into the following sections:

1. A general overview of the area of concern.
2. Voices of The Collective that highlight the concerns and experiences of staff of color.
3. Perceptions/Experiences. We use the term "perception" to describe how we understand and interpret experiences which are based on observations and personal incidents. We recognize that not every negative interaction or every decision made is intentional or malicious in nature against staff of color. However, many of us have shared similar, reoccurring experiences that perpetuate the *perception* that CLS is not as committed to the development and success of staff of color as they are to white staff.
4. Impact. We use the term "impact" to describe how one experience or phenomena influences another. When staff of color hold ongoing, un-addressed perceptions about CLS's commitment to their professional development and success, there

is a direct *impact* on their performance and morale which in turn, affects CLS as a whole.

5. Structures/practices to examine. We use the terms "structures/practices" to describe (both formal and informal) systems by which CLS operates and makes decisions. For every issue we discuss, we have identified an organizational structure or practice that allows, or at the very least, sustains these issues.

A. OFFICE CULTURE

1. Overview

In a June 2014 article in *American Lawyer* discussing racism in the legal profession (Chen 2014), Vivian Chen wrote,

What makes the legal field so impenetrable, I think, is that lawyers particularly those in major firms believe that they are intellectually superior. Firms promote the cult of cerebrals, preaching that only the brightest and most tenacious will win the prize. To some members of the establishment, minorities don't quite fit the bill. And so this myth of meritocracy creates a closed, self-satisfied, slow-evolving club that tends to admit members who are carbon copies of those already there.

It would be unfair to ignore CLS's efforts over the past few years to address issues of implicit bias such as offering several trainings on the subject, offering lunchtime series on issues affecting marginalized groups, and forming committees to look at professional development and other issues of organizational importance through an "equity" lens. Despite these efforts, CLS must acknowledge that implicit bias is embedded within our organizational culture. Similarly, individual advocates might acknowledge that implicit bias exists, yet refuse to engage in any genuine self-reflection of how their actions perpetuate implicit biases against their nonwhite colleagues.

The Collective's experience and perception is that many white staff do not trust their nonwhite colleagues' skills and judgment, and are content with forming superficial relationships. As a result, it is hard to trust that our white colleagues have our best interest in mind or treat us as equals.

If CLS continues to use the practice of law as a tool to achieve justice for our clients, but refuses to reject the parts of the practice that are oppressive to its nonwhite staff, its efforts to pursue race equity are insincere and will continue to be ineffective.

2. Voices of Staff of Color

Section removed. Staff of color give actual accounts of how the existing office culture dynamics have impacted them.

3. Experiences/Perceptions

As a result of the above experiences by staff of color, the effects are:

- Feeling that white attorneys invalidate the ideas of staff of color.
- Observing management and leadership automatically go to white staff members for help with an issue when a staff person of color may have much more experience and knowledge in that area.
- White attorneys are not required to prove their skills or earn the trust of other attorneys, and instead, it is assumed that white attorneys are inherently more skilled and worthy of being trusted than attorneys of color.
- Frustration at being micromanaged and not allowed to direct own projects.
- Feeling that new attorneys of color are treated like students, whereas white attorneys that join the program are treated as colleagues/equals by other white attorneys.

4. Impact on staff of color and ultimately, CLS

- Hard to integrate/develop authentic relationships.
- Distrust that white colleagues have best interest in mind.
- Not tapping into talent of attorneys/legal assistants/paralegals of color.

5. Structure

- Organization ideals do not align with recruitment and retention practices.
- Environment of meritocracy is perpetuated.

B. LEADERSHIP AND PROFESSIONAL DEVELOPMENT OPPORTUNITIES

1. Overview

CLS as an organization has recently begun to demonstrate a commitment to leadership development and diversifying our leadership staff. However, it is important to note that leadership development is not just the formal practice of setting benchmarks for each staff member, but it is also formed in the informal and formal relationships we develop with our colleagues through mentor/mentee relationships. In this vein, we have witnessed resistance to long-term strategic mentoring, and a culture that fosters impatience, perfectionism, and assimilation, rather than helping staff of color develop their unique talents. It appears that many in leadership are not comfortable with mentoring attorneys of color or do not know how to do it in an effective manner. As staff of color, connecting on a mentorship level can be extremely difficult when leadership is visibly uncomfortable with connecting with personalities that are not similar to their own.

2. Voices of Staff of Color

Section removed. Staff of color give personal accounts of CLS's practices related to cultivating leadership and professional development opportunities have impacted them.

3. Experiences/Perceptions

As a result of the above experiences by staff of color, the effects are:

- Developed feelings of inadequacy.
- Feeling undervalued and talents not being acknowledged.
- Emotional exhaustion.
- Self-doubt and questioning of one's own abilities and talents.

4. Impact on staff of color and ultimately, CLS

- Staff of color are not given an opportunity to develop into leaders/experts.
- Stunts/shuts down professional development which affects organizational knowledge base.
- High/frequent turnover of staff of color.
- Lack of diverse voices and opinions that can enhance overall program effectiveness, efficiency, and culture.

5. Structure

- Lack of clear goals as it relates to equity, access and opportunity for staff of color.
- Lack of evaluation/training of managers that ensure that equity/leadership priorities are
- being enforced organization-wide.
- Lack of transparency regarding pathways/opportunities for leadership.

- Reactionary decision-making.
- Lack of mentorship, as well as lack of institutionalized mentorship.

C. HIRING PROCESS

1. Overview

CLS lacks a clear hiring process, which is a concern to many staff of color.

Additionally, The Collective is concerned that CLS lacks a formal and effective recruitment process. CLS should be well-known within all communities and organizations throughout the State. However, CLS often fails to establish and maintain relationships with a wide range of groups that may be a source of potential employees. For example, it has limited relationships with the Black, Native American, Asian, and other minority bar associations in Washington, and rarely conducts outreach to these groups when a new job is posted. It also does not sufficiently engage in regular outreach to law schools and these same groups' student associations to create awareness and access to CLS, and a deeper pool of diverse candidates for CLS to choose from when hiring staff or interns. These are the types of structural issues that CLS needs to address when trying to avoid the same results with regards to the population of applicants who generally become aware of CLS positions.

Finally, The Collective is concerned about integration and retention of new hires. The hiring process does not end with the hiring of a candidate. CLS has either failed to consider or to effectively implement the important step of providing the newly hired employee with the appropriate tools, support, and training to effectively integrate that person into the program and cultivate his or her ability to be successful at CLS. Absent this step, employees can become isolated, discouraged, and frustrated. This can impact the retention of staff, intra-office relationships, employee potential, and program productivity. This problem is often magnified with staff of color.

2. Voices of Staff of Color

Section removed. This section gave the accounts of staff of color and their experiences of CLS's recruitment process.

3. Experiences/Perceptions

As a result of the above experiences by staff of color, the effects are:

- Feeling that white attorneys do not think that interns and externs of color bring value to the program.
- Confusion about how staff are recruited, selected and integrated.
- Feeling left out due to decisions affecting projects being made at higher levels without the input of the project group, which is where most staff of color are.

4. Impact on staff of color and ultimately, CLS

- CLS misses out on diverse talent, respect, and expertise.
- Staff of color do not disclose the actual reasons for leaving CLS; therefore, CLS lacks vital feedback for improving retention of staff of color.
- No change in status quo for those in leadership positions.
- Low morale and not valuing work.

5. Structure

- No institutionalized commitment to mentoring staff of color.
- No transparency or uniformity in the hiring process.

D. PROBLEM SOLVING OF EMPLOYEE CONCERNS

1. Overview

Race is often difficult to discuss. Even using the word "racist" tends to cause a great deal of discomfort. Because many concerns raised by staff of color may be perceived with an undercurrent of race, some staff of color are left with limited options including refusing to address the issue. Additionally, CLS has no formalized policies for addressing employee complaints, which can lead to arbitrary and inconsistent solutions to problems.

Furthermore, when CLS engages in staff discussions concerning these issues and how race plays a role, or discusses how CLS can better promote racial justice, the discussion often veers away from race, including white staff opting out of the conversation by stating how uncomfortable they are with the discussion, and insisting on a certain framework for discussing race. The effect of this framework is to put the discussion either on hold or present it as a dry academic discourse. Instead of addressing race "head-on," many white staff will often address race-related issues by wrongly referring to and analogizing race to other types of discrimination and oppression that staff are more comfortable discussing or more familiar in their own experiences, such as those related to sexuality, gender, disability, or age. Not only is this insulting to staff of color (and hopefully the entire organization), but it is an entirely ineffective approach for solving CLS's race-related problems. Race is a different and unique social construct and should not be viewed or addressed through a different construct's lens.

2. Voices of Staff of Color

Section removed. This section outlines staff of color's experiences as it relates to raising concerns especially related to race or perceived racism.

3. Experiences/Perceptions

As a result of the above experiences by staff of color, the effects are:

- Feeling unsafe to share real feelings with management and leadership and move to solution.
- Frustration of having to exert extra energy in "how" things are said, versus the value of "what" is said.
- Dejection that many staff (both white and nonwhite) will not speak up about obvious race inequities for various reasons.
- Apathy about race-related issues never truly being resolved.

4. Impact on staff of color and ultimately, CLS

- Distrust and fear between all staff.
- No safe space to address concerns on race or other sensitive issues.
- General discomfort (and some ignorance) about issues of race as a conduit to ONE CLS.
- No opportunity for real transformational dialogue to occur between white and nonwhite staff as no one is speaking up.

5. Structure

- Maintain power dynamic structure at CLS.
- Most staff in power are white and control decision making.
- Different locations make it difficult to know how these issues are playing out in other offices.
- Gossip culture among management and leadership.

II. Proposed Solutions for CLS

Based on the aforementioned experiences, impacts and structures, The Collective has identified some solutions that we believe would go a long way toward actualizing our vision of ONE CLS.

The following list of solutions were generated by The Collective to address the structural issues that are preventing the realization of ONE CLS. They are categorized by the four key areas of office culture, leadership and professional development opportunities, hiring process, and problem solving of employee concerns.

Area of concern	Proposed Solution
Office Culture	• Evaluate those people in leadership to make sure they are following CLS's values and include questions regarding race and equity in evaluation process. • Mandatory equity training for staff in leadership positions. • Formalize/institutionalize The Collective as an official group within CLS for staff of color to have ongoing dialogue; seek support from one another; aid in successful integration of new staff of color; and to provide insight to CLS on issues of race and equity.
Leadership Development Opportunities	• Formalized Mentorship Program to show a commitment to mentorship for all staff. • Finalize the Leadership Development Guide and the Professional Development documents for attorneys and legal assistants created by the Equity Project over a year ago to make sure that all staff are developing the skills that CLS wants to see. • CLS does not follow a set, fair, and equitable way to learn about staff experience and skills; we need to stop talking about professional development and leadership standards and start implementing them.
Hiring Practices	• Establish a Uniform Hiring Process. • Transparency in hiring; in selecting candidates; in the weight of equity when hiring; and in learning about the staff of color's experience and skills.

Problem Solving of Employee Concerns	• Institutionalize role of the Director of Equity in managing employee issues. • A staff of color (such as the Equity Director) should do separate exit interviews for staff of color.

III. CONCLUSION

Racial challenges are difficult and the Collective thanks the CLS for the opportunity to explore and present the above issues. We acknowledge that CLS has been and will continue to be at the forefront in its advocacies and it is not our intent to demean the work of CLS or single out any one person in our discussion. We further acknowledge that moving toward ONE CLS is challenging but appreciate the cooperative spirit of CLS in moving toward that goal. The Collective's intent is to keep that momentum and move CLS internally, as well as externally, to a new level through honest and meaningful dialogue.

The Collective welcomes all comments and feedback from CLS.

Chen, Vivia. "The Diversity Crisis: Time to Call It Racism?" *The American Lawyer*, 5 June 2014, www.americanlawyer.com/id=1202656369463/The-Diversity-Crisis-Time-to-Call-It-Racism.

Poverty and Race: Deepening our Understanding of Structural Marginalization, John Powell, Vol. 22, No. 5 • September/October 2013.

Racialequitytools.org. (2018). [online] Available at: http://www.racialequitytools.org/images/uploads/N._White_Culture_Handout.pdf [Accessed 17 Oct. 2018].

Now that you've gotten a chance to see the letter, here is a snapshot of the framework we used and why.

Section	Rationale
Opening of letter	The opening sets the tone for the "spirit" of the letter. After reading the opening, readers should have a clear idea of the intention and commitment of the group. This was one of the areas that The Collective spent the most time as this section is the only section where it represents the voices of all members. The other areas are more individualistic in nature.
Body of Letter	
General overview of each of your issues	Sets up the context of the issue you are concerned with in a clear, measured voice such that the reader has an understanding of the area and why it needs to be changed.
Tangible Examples	This is the only section where we decided to allow for more emotive language and tone as it gives authentic accounts from people and moves the issue from the theoretical to the experiential. Also, some people need an "example" to more fully understand the issue as you see it, so this section is important.
Perceptions/Experiences	Recognizing that people say or do things unintentionally, we felt it was important to not only identify the experience but the perception that it leaves. This is especially important when people say, "I didn't mean it" as a way to deflect from their actions. While people can deny their actions/intentions, no one can deny how another "perceives" their actions.
Impact	Share not only the impact on the person, but the impact on the organization when these issues go unchecked.
Structures/Practices	By identifying the structures and practices issues at play, the organization can better see themes and areas to evaluate.
Solutions	As the people most impacted, often times staff of color are best suited to propose solutions to address issues. Also, this positions them as thought partners and collaborators in transforming the organization.

E. Integrating Race Equity Work

Many organizations attempt to integrate race equity into their work without ensuring *psychological safety*. In the early stages, we were heavily focused on changing the process, it soon became very clear that without doing more work to ensure organizational trust and safety, #OneCLS would remain a "great idea" and never become a reality. A psychologically safe environment is one in which people feel safe to share ideas, ask questions, and make mistakes without fear of humiliation or punishment. This does not happen overnight, and CLS *continues* to work on this. This can also be especially challenging in the legal profession where it's all about doing things right, and appearing to have it all together. I'll share more about the steps we took to create psychological safety, but first I think it's important to talk about some of the challenges many organizations face when doing race equity work.

Some of these challenges will be pretty obvious, and others will completely throw leaders off guard if they are not aware of them. The following six challenges are a compilation of both personal observations and shared stories from fellow race equity consultants.

1. Fear of Change

The one constant thing in life (and organizations) is change. Some things, like budget, are out of our control and can force changes that organizations need to react to. But there are other changes that organizations *choose* to make – like institutionalizing equity into their organizational fabric. Either way, people generally resist change and this resistance can weigh heavy on the head of the leaders. Also, because this change was related to a subject as anxiety producing as race/race equity, we had to be especially deliberate in how we thought things through. It took a lot of adjusting and re-framing to get into some kind of rhythm where we could gain some traction. This required a great deal of humility and vulnerability on Merf's part to move with the "will of the people", which wasn't always easy.

Speaking of humility, as a leader, you'll need a great deal of it because this work (and any kind of organizational change) is largely based on learning, being transparent, and being willing to make adjustments.

What many leaders think	What we learned	What we did
I can just tell my staff that "We are now going to prioritize race equity in our work" and people will change.	Change often requires a shift in culture which can't be changed with a simple communication.	We delivered many, many messages, all with a consistent theme and vision. We also worked as a leadership body to develop consistent talking points about this shared vision.
"We've been doing this for a year. We should be way further ahead by now." Or "It seems like things are actually getting worse! What gives?"	Slow, steady and CONSISTENT wins this race.	At no point was it ever a consideration that we were going to abandon our efforts in this work. We were also transparent in how much this work can suck sometimes and that's just part of it. We never tried to pretend that "everything was just fine" when it wasn't. We spoke to the discomfort and anxiety.
I can do this work with the same people and the same structures.	The structures and/ or people will need to adjust to do this work. Trying to implement new ideas with the same people, attitudes, behaviors and structures will not work.	Some people left who were not aligned with this work. This happens. We also implemented several structural changes that we'll address in a later chapter.

| Why are people so resistant to this work? I thought they "wanted" to do race equity work? | Embrace resistance as a normal, human reaction. Even the most committed and supportive staff members may have some resistance when asked to change. | We incorporated several opportunities for staff to give input along the way as buy-in was a key aspect in moving this work forward. Also, we were consistent about messaging the importance of *normalizing* resistance and conflict related to change. |

Finally, and probably one of the most important factors in managing fears and resistance to change is making sure to have effective *resistance managers* in place. These are people who are put in place to anticipate and handle resistance of the staff during change. I believe that the key is to *expect* resistance and conflict, and then make sure to have the right players in place to handle it when it happens. Ideally, resistance management could look similar to this:

Senior Leadership/Leadership Team - The voice of change. Keeps a consistent message of the vision. Acknowledges resistance and makes a compelling case for the need to stay on course during times of change.

Middle Management - The voice of support. These are the managers who lead teams of staff and serve as a conduit for the Director's voice. They will manage resistance by openly, actively and consistently re-articulating *and modeling* the Director's message and vision to their teams.

Change Manager - The voice of action. This person, (my role in this case) is on the frontlines of the resistance. This person keeps the ball moving down the field and does the legwork of implementing and managing the practical pathways to fulfill the Director's vision of race equity.

If I could highlight anything from this section, it is the need for leadership to *normalize* resistance to change. **Preparing** people upfront for resistance shows that as an organization you are capable and supportive of people having their own experiences throughout the process. **Managing** the change with consistent communication and opportunities for staff to give input promotes clarity and buy-in. Finally, formally **revisiting and reflecting** on race equity work throughout the lifecycle provides a framework to continuously deal with resistance or fears that may be active or lie dormant.

2. Checking Power and Privilege

When we first began race equity work, I was still technically the Development Director. But when I assumed the role of Equity Director and joined the leadership team, all of a sudden, I had power and privilege that I never accounted for. So, when some Collective members began to respond or relate to me differently, it wasn't clear to me why. Personally, all seemed well, but professionally, they now saw me as *one of them,* which shifted the power dynamics and my participation with The Collective.

While I had come to really care about The Collective members and wanted to continue being a part of the group, I had to be accountable for my new role as leadership and how that affected their ability to be open and free to have candid conversations.

I made the mistake of forgetting that I had access to certain information (power), and a meaningful voice at the leadership table (privilege). First, when Collective members were expressing their frustrations related to CLS or their position in particular, I responded through my points of privilege and not as a supportive Collective member. Secondly, I would impose expectations on The Collective based on *my own experience at CLS* which had always been good, forgetting that others had different experiences with CLS in the past. I can see how that could be frustrating for people who had been there more than twice as long as I had and felt I didn't appreciate their past experiences. Finally, I found myself getting resentful that Collective members didn't really see all the work that the leadership team was doing to make CLS a better, more inclusive, transparent, and rewarding place to work. But how could they? Staff only see what is shared by leadership and not the work behind the scenes.

I think many organizational leaders/leadership teams, don't do a good enough job of putting themselves in the shoes of the staff they are serving. This is a huge mistake and has a demoralizing effect on morale. This furthers my argument of having an internal person doing this work who understands the needs of staff and can legitimately represent their interests.

The unique thing about CLS' leadership team was that it was comprised of seven individuals. One white man, two white women, two black women, one Asian American woman, and one Latino man. We represented a broad range of racial diversity. But I think *more* importantly, four of us came from non-leadership roles which strongly influenced how we thought through challenges related to staff experiences and perceptions.

3. Manage the Optics

There are two kinds of *optics* people are familiar with in this work. The "optics" to stakeholders in which organizations want to "look like" they are doing the work, but actually aren't doing the deep work it takes to shift an organizational culture. This is also known as the "check the box" method. The second form of optics that most leaders tend to ignore are the *internal optics*, which is related to how staff *interprets* the decisions and actions of leadership.

For the most part, people are meaning-making machines that are designed to protect ourselves. When an event occurs, we observe it, assign meaning to it, (figure out what it *means* about us, or how it *affects* us) and then begin to behave in accordance to that meaning – not necessarily the facts. Also, it has been my experience that many people don't investigate their assumptions, instead they react to them as a truth. This then leads to gossip, or as Merf called it, "The CLINC" (Columbia Legal Informal Network of Communication).

The CLINC moved like lightning speed around CLS, so we tried to stay ahead of it by spending a lot of time upfront figuring out what we needed to report out in our announcements. Over time, I'd say that as long as we included the following information, we could, to some degree mitigate the effects of misinterpretations and confusion that activated the CLINC.

1. **Why the change was made.** Lack of awareness of why things happen is probably the number one cause of organizational mistrust and tension.

2. **How this will affect the person's/team's job role and security.** People don't have to make assumptions about how it affects them, if you tell them. Also, it sends a message that you are in tune to the concerns of the people who will most likely be affected by a potential change.

3. **Acknowledgment of staff concerns or past failures.** It's not enough to say, *"we are going to do equity work and here is my new vision"*, but it is equally important to say, *"I recognize that we have tried this before. We did this thing and that thing and we missed the mark. Here is what we are doing differently now..."* Like most things, when you try to step over past failures and just create anew, staff have no way to discern how this time will be different and may automatically distrust it.

A final note on managing optics: how people interpret anything is ultimately an individual phenomenon. Of course we can turn to research to help us gain a broader understanding of some of the root causes of how and why groups perceive things the way they do, but the best and most effective (not always the most efficient) way I found to manage optics is through personal conversations with staff. Merf scheduled individual 15 or 30-minute conversations with every staff member twice per year--specifically to talk about race, giving them an opportunity to share their concerns. She would also report back to the leadership team after her staff calls were completed and share any themes or concerns that we needed to be mindful of.

4. People leave and that's ok

Whenever an organization is taking on a new initiative that causes a shift in the way things are done, or in organizational priorities, expect some people to leave.

There is often a subset of staff in most organizations who benefit from "the way things used to be" and don't want to lose those benefits, so they may likely try to sabotage efforts and/or end up leaving the organization.

However, there are others who may not necessarily be aligned to the new organizational vision, *but want or need to stay*. These folks fall into two categories:

1. **They go along to get along.** Perhaps they love their work/ the organization and don't want to leave. In some cases, it's not financially feasible to leave. Perhaps they see the value, but simply don't want to do the work of race equity as it gets in the way of "their real work". These people are usually more passive in their resistance.
2. **They actively resist.** Active resistance can range from criticizing the work/leadership, to disrupting the efforts of the work, spreading rumors or making false claims--especially race-related claims. I've seen organizations go through tremendous turmoil under these circumstances, and can't stress enough that working effectively with staff who are engaged in this behavior should be a top priority as it has a serious impact on the organizational safety, sanctity and stability. As an aside, in the event that this actively resistant staff is a staff of

color, I think it's important that leaders think critically about whether or not it's more important to keep misaligned staff in order to avoid the negative optics of letting go of a person of color, versus doing what is best for the organization.

Staff of color. I am compelled to add that because many leaders hold a racialized analysis of behavior, there are often times when people of color behave/react in a way that is considered aggressive or resistant, whereas their white counterparts are labeled as assertive or confident. Staff of color are more likely to be addressed with *punitive* measures, as opposed to white staff who are more likely given *restorative* opportunities. So, it is absolutely critical for leaders to be discerning and able to check their racial bias.

Here is where I'll make a quick plug for having a multi-racial leadership team, so that there can be an objective/subjective analysis of the staff's behavior. While Merf was actively committed to developing her racial analysis, she admittedly relied on the feedback and input from her team to help her think through the most effective decision for staff. For example, as a woman of color, there may have been some insight that I could contribute through the lens of a Black woman that would help her see things from a different angle. The key here is for leaders to be able to have a wider lens to evaluate staff, their staff's behavior, and the best approach to respond to it. This is best done with a diverse leadership team who can bring broad perspectives, and a leader who *truly* considers their input.

With that said, not everyone is going to fit in with the mission and vision of your organization. I work with consultants around the nation who are coaching leaders on how to effectively manage staff members who are essentially bringing harm to their organizations. In some cases, these staff members are in leadership roles which makes it worse because they tend to hire people who share *their* vision, rather than the Director's/organization's vision. This only perpetuates harmful cycles and is why I argue for *cutting ties sooner rather than later*. However, many leaders, understandably, want to exhaust every option before terminating someone. But keeping toxic staff members on board often ends up costing more time and money on the back end dealing with consulting costs or even legal fees.

5. Setbacks/Comebacks

Let me first say that there will likely be a moment when you question why you ever started this work and you'll want to quit. If you don't experience this moment, you're probably not doing the work. At the very least, there will be setbacks. You'll feel like you are making headway, people are communicating more, the affinity groups seem to be gelling and them something will happen that will cause people to question everything.

There was a challenging situation that occurred with a staff member of color. I can tell you having been a part of the leadership team, that this situation had nothing to do with this staff member's race, but rather their performance. It was a clear call that I (and the rest of leadership) was fully aware of and agreed it needed to be handled in a certain way. It was an unfortunate decision that needed to be made and even though we were aware of the potential racialized optics of the decision, we all agreed it was the best decision to be made.

Had I not been a part of the leadership team, I would have been highly suspicious of this being a race issue. This situation taught me that that there are some times when you have to weigh the risks between a *negative perception* about a decision, or real harm being brought your organization.

This is where honesty and transparency come in. I would say, acknowledge the breakdowns. If you commit to something and don't do it, acknowledge that you didn't do it. If you try something and it doesn't work, acknowledge that you missed the mark and let people know the new plan. CLS staff, and I'm sure others, are very keen and aware when things go awry, so not acknowledging breakdowns makes them think that leadership is either not aware of what is going on in the organization, or don't care. Either way, trust in leadership will erode.

When setbacks happen, people will likely say, "See, we haven't really made much progress. Here we are again". All that I know to do is to own it, clean it up and repeat your message of hope and commitment toward this work.

II

Where Social Meets Justice

A. Overview

Shifting a culture can't be achieved through a top-down mandate. It can only happen through the hearts and minds of the people who share a perception of "this is how we do it", or this is "the (insert your organization here) way". A leader can mandate compliance, but they can't enforce trust, optimism, or meaningful engagement.

—*Dr Michelle Majors*

If you recall in the Collective Letter, there were solutions that were proposed that fell into four different categories. These were solutions recommended by The Collective that they believed would address many of the challenges that were raised in the letter. CLS's continued work is based on strengthening these four key areas and answering the corresponding questions:

1. **Managing Conflict** - Are we a punitive or restorative organization and who do we deem worthy of redemption?
2. **Office Culture** - Does the culture of our organization promote psychological safety, respect, and the ability to make mistakes?
3. **Leadership/Professional Development** - Do staff members know how to be successful and are they equally afforded opportunities to develop skills?
4. **Hiring Practices** - Are we intentional about ensuring that our employment opportunities reach a diverse pool of candidates, does the selection process include diverse voices within the organization and are new employees successfully integrated into the organization?

The entire organization was divided into four groups to analyze and create implementation plans for the above categories. Again, these groups were comprised of both people of color and white staff who worked *together*. Moving forward I will refer to the groups as "The Conflict Team", "The Office Culture Team", etc.

Interestingly, these four categories seemed to be evenly divided between a "social" and a "justice" orientation. Our *office culture* and how we *manage conflict* was strongly influenced by our **social** norms and interactions with each other. Our approach to addressing these two categories was to focus on relationship building and personal connection.

On the other hand, *professional development* and *hiring practices* were more technical in nature and provoked more structural or system changes. These changes pushed us to ensure our practices were even-handed, fair and transparent and **just.** It was clear that we would need to focus on our processes and structures so that people were clear about how to be successful at CLS.

The Challenge

After the Collective letter went out, CLS was now faced with an *opportunity* to thoughtfully react to the letter and in particular the proposed solutions outlined by The Collective. Many questions arose. How do we actually implement these solutions? Should The Collective members spearhead the efforts to ensure solution implementation since it was their experience/letter? Is it fair for people of color to bear the burden of both identifying AND "fixing" the issues that affect them? What about white allies getting engaged? Should *they* take the lead in solidarity and support of The Collective? If they jump in too aggressively would that send off the "white savior" alarms creating further strife?

The Solutions

While some argued that The Collective members should take the lead on implementing the solutions, I felt strongly that we were sitting on a huge opportunity to advance the concept of #OneCLS. By working side-by-side, white allies and collective members, to implement the solutions, we were actively demonstrating unity and a shared commitment to creating an equitable and just organization.

In March of 2017, we divided our entire organization (cross-racially, demographically, hierarchically) into four groups. Each of these groups would *own* one of the four categories listed and work together to propose a plan to transform that category. Two months later, at #OneCLS Day 2017, all four groups gave presentations to all staff. They presented their suggestions and implementation strategies for transforming CLS's culture, managing conflict, recruiting, hiring, and retaining staff and streamlining professional/leadership development processes.

I have had several people ask me about the specific changes we made. Some of the changes that we made were specific to the letter, while others were made simply due to our deepening awareness of the gaps that we needed to fill. The good, and perhaps not so good news about doing this work, is that the more you learn and grow, the more you see all of the many, many...many ways that you still need to grow. So, we found ourselves constantly fine tuning and adding new ways to expand our range of competence. For example, for our annual fundraising event, we had been using the same caterer for at least four of the five years that we held this event. I was part of the team that planned and organized the event and for a few reasons, we made the decision to procure another caterer. We went through what we felt was a pretty extensive reflection process to think through our decision and to find another vendor. We asked around in our circles, we searched the web for vendors who held the same social justice mission as the prior caterer and came up with one caterer. When Merf found out that we selected another caterer she inquired about why we made the decision, and after looking up the new caterer she was displeased by the lack of diversity of their staff. She challenged us all to think about striking that balance between our commitment to diversity, equity and procuring vendors who reflect the client communities we serve and fiscal prudence. In that meeting, it was decided that we needed to create a values-based screening process for our vendors. The next day, I reached out to the white allies' group and The Collective members to come together to create such a document that would ensure that our vendors not only align with our values, but don't have any prior or current issues related to labor/employment practices, or discriminatory policies or practices, etc.

There were quite a few instances like this where we discovered gaps and took immediate action. But as for the more notable changes, here are some of the accomplishments we made in a little over 18 months. Most of these will be addressed in later chapters.

Office Culture	Conflict Management
• Completed the Equity Director Job description based on needs and recommendations of staff • Officialized caucus groups • Voted on and finalized organizational **agreements** that guide our treatment of one another; and our **values** that undergird our agreements • Institutionalized OneCLS Day as an annual event to deepen our equity work and connect with one another for the sole purpose of discussing race and our progress • Training Calendar - Expanded our monthly calendar to go beyond advocacy related skills, to include equity, communication and relationship building competencies	• Implemented Restorative Justice (RJ) as a new model to manage conflict • Established a RJ curriculum including monthly reflection themes for the purpose of encouraging dialogue among staff that would aid in better communication during times of conflict • Revamped our sexual discrimination and harassment policy • Amended language in our Board policies and Collective Bargaining Agreement

Professional/Leadership Development	Hiring
• Re-tooled performance evaluation process to ensure transparency and consistency • Created the CLS Mentorship Program • Established an organization wide Talent Bank which served as a repository of staff talents and skills to share with other staff members • Re-tooled the exit interview process with a commitment to use the data to improve CLS policies/practices • Adopted new language in CLS's Collective Bargaining Agreement to distinguish between Professional Development and Performance Evaluations	• Consistency in Advertising salaries • Included Equity questions for applicants to answer and submit along with their application materials to gain perspective on applicant fluency on equity • Overhauled the entire hiring process to ensure that an equity lens is applied to each step of the process • Established clear and unified internal hiring process for staff to have priority for new vacancies • Adjusted language on job descriptions to highlight equity as a preferred and highly valued competence

Advocacy/Other
• Our Race Equity Toolkit helps us think through the cases we take and how they impact our communities. • Committed to establishing an evaluation matrix to measure effectiveness of our efforts. • The Vendor Equity Toolkit (V.E.T.) was conceived to ensure that we are selecting values-based vendors who are aligned with CLS mission/vision.

I believe that one of the best things we did was to work together in the implementation process. While race is a difficult conversation to have at face value, it was easier to see and reflect on the different racial perspectives of staff of color and white staff when working together on issues that affect our organization. For example, the "hiring practices" team was making a determination about whether or not to list the salary range for the positions we were recruiting for. This discussion opened up dialogue about how people of color react to a job listing when the salary is listed, versus when the salary is not listed. Or, while thinking through mentorship, The Collective members felt it was important to match new attorneys of color with more senior attorneys of color. That made sense in the beginning, but after working with the "leadership/professional development team", staff (both staff of color and white staff) recognized that the most senior attorneys (those that have been here 20 years plus) were all white. This meant that new attorneys of color weren't gaining access to the depth of knowledge that these senior attorneys could offer. As a result, this made us think more about the composition of our organization ensuring that we not only built a more diverse staff, but that all people had access the knowledge and wisdom of our more senior attorneys.

Another benefit of working together was that people reported that they got to know each other better in this process. With offices around the state, this was a rare opportunity to work together and be able to strengthen relationships across the organization.

Our entire organization rallied around this letter and actively engaged in implementing the solutions that would address the concerns that the Collective raised. Once all of the solutions and implementation plans were presented at #OneCLS Day 2017, I, as the Equity Director began the process of implementing each solution one by one. The final solution was implemented in May of 2018.

Next, we will examine some of the solutions and how their implementation has helped us think differently about how we interact with one another (the social work); and helped us create structures that promote an equitable and transparent organization (the justice/structural work).

B. The Social Work

"Our individual greatness best shines in the light of our shared collective values.—Dr. Michelle Majors

social adjective so·cial \ 'sō-shəl \

a: tending to form cooperative and interdependent relationships with others

John Dovidio is a professor at Yale University who has studied issues of social power and social relations, both between groups and between individuals. His work explores both conscious (explicit) and unconscious (implicit) influences on how people think about, feel about, and behave toward others based on group membership.

Following is an excerpt of an interview with Dr. Dovidio and the American Psychological Association in a 2009 interview entitled, *"Five Questions for John Dovidio, PhD"*:

APA: *What are the key psychological factors that shape racial attitudes, and how ingrained are those attitudes? Can people with deep-seated racial prejudice ever completely change those attitudes?*

Dr. Dovidio: *Attitudes develop with the accumulation of experience and associations over time. They are inherently functional – they help us orient ourselves to others and the environment in ways perceived to benefit us. The world would be chaos if we changed our attitudes toward people and objects too easily. Thus, attitudes typically evolve slowly, often becoming more complex and nuanced over time; rapid, wholesale change in attitudes is rare. One of the best ways to change attitudes is through intergroup contact. Attitudes are not simply about the way you think about* *a group; they are also about how you feel about a group. In America, whites have been able to change their minds about racism faster than they have been able to change their deep-seated, and often unconscious, feelings. The vast majority of white Americans currently know we should be non-prejudiced and egalitarian. But the emotional impact, the "gut" impact, that race has on people still lags behind. So, to truly change attitudes at their core requires direct interracial experiences that are positive and personal, and which replace feelings of fear, anxiety and with those of empathy, connection and respect for members of another group.*

What Dr. Dovidio is referring to lays at the heart of our work at CLS--creating opportunities for people to connect and learn and grow from one another; and while he is referencing white people, his answer is also relevant for people of color who have *instinctively* developed a mistrust for white people. The only way to move through this mistrust and the "gut" impact that Dr. Dovidio is referencing, is to "engage in interracial experiences that are positive and personal", and I would add *authentic*.

This is the "social" work of equity.

As you may recall the Collective letter was divided into four categories. Two of which were strongly tied to our ***social environment*** and the call for civility, respect, connection and cohesiveness. These two categories were *Office Culture* and *Conflict Management*.

1. Office Culture

CLS has a strong organizational mission to achieve social and economic justice for all. However, The Collective raised concerns that this mission did not always align with the true workplace culture; and without addressing the biases that are deeply embedded within the organizational fabric, the work toward equity would be ineffective at best, insincere at worst. As a result of CLS's office culture, the following issues were experienced by many staff of color:

- Lack of appreciation of diverse experiences and perspectives
- Hard to integrate/develop authentic relationships
- Not feeling like POC voice/experiences are heard/validated
- Lack of belongingness
- Isolation (cultural/spatial/geographic)

We decided to start caucusing so that we could create a safe environment where we could ideally address these issues.

a. Affinity Group/Caucusing

In creating strategies and frameworks for our caucusing groups, we referred to Crossroads, an organizing, training, and consulting firm to support institutions striving to dismantle racism. In an article by Crossroads entitled, *"Racial Identity Caucusing: A Strategy for Building Anti-Racist Collectives"*, the framework of our caucusing work is outlined.

> *Racial identity in the United States is not shaped in a neutral environment. The identities of People of Color form in response to racial oppression, and the identities of Whites form in response to racial superiority. These two identity dynamics manifest in a complex range of attitudes and behaviors that support and perpetuate the racist paradigm in this country. In order to work together to dismantle individual, institutional, and cultural racism, People of Color and Whites must understand how these identity dynamics operate in specific institutional settings, and devise strategies to overcome the barriers and oppression that are created by them.* - Crossroads

I believe that caucusing is vital to the healing of organizational racial divides by allowing staff to share knowledge, experiences, and their unique understanding of the world. When done thoughtfully and strategically, not only can caucusing shift the culture of the organization, but it can be powerful and personally transformative for the caucus members.

There are two caucus groups at CLS – The Collective and The White Allies group.

The Collective

The Collective was created in 2016 when 18 CLS staff of color came together to highlight the historical racial climate and concerns within CLS with the ultimate goal of establishing an equitable, safe, and transparent organization for all employees. The ongoing work of The Collective is to further support CLS in fostering a culture that values all people as reflected by our policies, practices and interactions.

The purpose of The Collective is to:

1. Strengthen the organizational culture by creating a safe space for staff of color to come together, share, affirm experiences and offer support of one another; and,
2. Support in the recruitment, retention, development and progression of staff of color at CLS.

One of the highlights of my time at CLS was working with The Collective. I really believe in the spirit and commitment of this group. In the beginning I was an active part of The Collective and attended all meetings. But as the Equity Director, it got confusing as to whether or not my work, or allegiance was to people of color, rather than the entire organization. My work was in the advancement of #OneCLS so I decided to discontinue my participation with The Collective to make it clear that my role was to serve and support *all* staff. This was pretty upsetting for me, but it was the right decision because I took up a lot of space in the facilitation and management of the group. Once I left the group, The Collective reinvented themselves in a way that made them stronger and more cohesive. One mistake affinity groups make is being led by one particular person, with a particular style and vision, and when that person leaves, the group loses momentum.

Finally, as The Collective's internal group identity expanded, so did their desire to impact CLS in new and innovative ways. For example, in the beginning there was a lot of time in meetings processing organizational issues and concerns, or venting. As they grew as a team, they began to process staff concerns with more deliberation and solution orientation. They also began exploring ideas like how to expand their voice in areas of fundraising, mentoring or hiring and recruitment efforts.

What is internalized oppression by people of color and how does caucusing help?

Crossroads defines internalized racist oppression as "a complex, multi-generational socialization process in which People of Color accept, believe and live out negative societal definitions."

Crossroads postulates that exploring how internalized oppression affects people of color, not only in our country but in our organizational work, is essential to truly dismantling institutional and cultural racism. The deep work of The Collective and other POC spaces is to consistently explore and confront how internalized oppression affects their personal attitudes and behavior. Crossroads has identified four areas that we should consistently examine:

- Personal - How do you perceive yourself?
- Intra-racial - How do you operate within your race group and/ or perceive others in your race group?
- Interracial - How do you interact with other race groups?
- Institutional - How do you operate in your organization, how do relate to power structures?

The Collective used articles and other media to generate dialogue that provoked the above questions. As humans, our perceptions, attitudes and beliefs are subconscious and many of us don't even know why we think the way we do, or act the way we act. Without a deliberate and safe way to interrogate our beliefs, we are doomed to continue making decisions that reinforce racists constructs, rather than challenge them--even as people of color.

Internalized oppression at play

Following are some actual examples of internalized oppression at play in caucus groups. They are a compilation of stories shared by other practitioners in this work, as well as my own reflections

- **Resentment by senior staff of color** – I was in a class where a young woman who identified as a third wave (1990s) feminist was embroiled in an argument with an older second wave (1960's) feminist. The second wave feminist resented how entitled, privileged and "uppity" these younger feminists were and she was appalled by the things they fought for like public breastfeeding, when there are more pressing issues like the wage gap between women and men. In this same way, some senior staff of color who experienced "real" inequities during their tenure can get resentful when other young staff of color bicker over things like office space, or the right to wear dreadlocks. Some senior staff of color have been around for a while and recall a time where racism was more overt and harsh. They became experts at "going along to get along", and have little patience for those who come into *their* organization and not only buck the system, but demand things that the senior staff of color never would have gotten, let alone asked for. In some cases, they excessively monitor and police the actions of newer staff. Or they complain to leadership about newer staff of color who they feel are "getting over" in ways they couldn't. I was told by one senior staff of color that I was "taking this equity shit too far". Instead of learning from each other, internalized oppression creates a divide between younger staff of color who can bring fresh ideas and innovation; and senior staff that bring wisdom and institutional knowledge.

- **Ulterior motives and advancing personal gains** – Sometimes people have ulterior motives and use the voice of the caucus group to leverage their personal motives. For example, if someone has an aim to secure a promotion within the organization, they can appeal to the caucus group claiming issues of race. If the caucus group is not astute, they can become emotionally swayed by this person and act collectively on their behalf. Once issues of race become a factor, many organizations will often cave to the pressure of the claim and give the wrongly motivated person what they want. This is a major reason why the caucus groups must have agreements about **what** they choose to react to and **process** for doing so. Internalized oppression leads people to believe that they can't be successful on the merits of their own gifts and talents and must manipulate others to get ahead.

- **Deflection** – Along the same lines as ulterior motives, this particular issue is less insidious in nature. There are some staff who may be having performance issues and they will use race to deflect from these issues. Doing organization wide race equity work can create an "egg-shell" effect where people, in particular white people, don't want to be viewed or called out as racist. This sets up the perfect storm when you have a white manager who is afraid to discipline their staff of color, especially when that staff member is one who is particularly outspoken about issues of race. In these instances, the staff's performance issues go unchecked or are blamed on a racial issue like, "this manager didn't like me, or support me because I'm Black". What makes this more frustrating is that there are legitimate issues of race-based discrimination that don't get taken as seriously because of such staff who cry wolf in an effort to deflect from their performance or other issues.

- **Staying in complaint mode** – When people who are oppressed don't see their power, they find power in their shared pain, i.e. complaining. I think this is due to an internalized belief that they truly have no agency to make a difference. One of my colleagues once called this the "comfort zone" for people of color. I didn't understand it at first, but they explained that just like white people sometimes don't want to confront certain aspects of their power and privilege, sometimes people of color get comfortable in this state because it's easier to complain about something than to fix it. For sure it feels safer to complain, than take the risk of calling something out and confronting it head on. I saw this in the early stages of The Collective. It just seemed that we'd get into a spiral of how bad things were and couldn't move to a place where we could see the power we really had to make a difference. It took time, structure and a consistent commitment to become a group that not only understands its power, but is committed to using it responsibly.

- **Lack of Accountability** – One thing that seems to be common among many caucus groups is the unwillingness to collectively "call in" members who have somehow gone rogue or are taking actions that don't necessarily reflect the views the entire group. This is internalized oppression at its finest – when the individuals of a group don't hold each other accountable to a particular standard that is reflective of their group. For people who have children, most of us would correct or redirect our child if we saw them acting in ways that don't positively reflect the family/societal norms. We do it because we care about the child and want them to be better. We do it because we know that our voice carries weight with that child and believe *that our guidance/support will make a difference.* Also, we do it because we don't want others under the impression that we think that their behavior is ok. Holding each other accountable is important for the sanctity, integrity, credibility and collective power of the group.

While there may have been rough patches, The Collective as a group has shown tremendous resilience and commitment to this work and each other. As far as The Collective's experience, I can't speak for individual members, but from my vantage point, I can see how much CLS has changed as a result of The Collective's voice and sense of agency related to organizational practices, policies and culture. I have also witnessed Collective members be more daring in their work, applying for and receiving positions that required them to stretch themselves.

An Interview with a Collective Member (CM)

Michelle: You have been part of The Collective from the very beginning. Can you talk about what your experience has been in general?

CM: In the past three years since The Collective has started, I've seen nothing but positive growth in it.

At an individual level, it has given me space to hear the different experiences of my colleagues, what they have gone through, how they have handled certain situations, how they felt about things afterward, and, the biggest positive impact for me, just how relatable a lot of these stories are.

We've all gone through them in a number of different ways and different situations, but they all carry those "ah-ha" moments where you say, "Oh, something similar has happened to me in the past." You get the sense of community and the sense of affirmation that your feelings are valid.

You have this space to just vent, to share your experiences with others, and not be worried about teaching someone how color works its way into everyday interactions. Also, once you've been able to work through those emotions, eventually you get to a point where – you, or someone else asks, is there anything you want to actually do about it?

Big or small, this group gives us a chance to get together and create connections that may not exist because we are separated by different offices statewide. It has been an absolute pleasure.

Michelle: You talked about some of the good things that have happened and what you witnessed over the last few years and we also hit some pretty rough patches. Can you talk to me about times where you felt like, "Wow! Was this really a good idea? Are we really serving our highest and best potential as a group?" You know, some of the questions that we grappled with in The Collective.

CM: The risk that any organization has when they start forming these "Collective" groups within itself is that you are getting people to share their experiences. I believe that most people would stay in isolation and go through different events or scenarios on their own. People would normally feel lost and question themselves. If any issue or problem ever makes it to the surface, it depends on how confident the individual is, where they find themselves in the hierarchy, how much authority or power they think they have, how much seniority they might have. I think people often decide to suffer in silence.

When you create these groups, the risk is that you have people driven by emotions without a process to deal with those emotions, how to recognize what space you're in at the moment. What do you do with people who have been in the organization for years and people who just joined the organization? That is where I found myself in the very beginning, I was just listening to a lot of stories of people being put down, people feeling ignored, and people feeling like they were not valued.

That's a lot to take in as a new member to the organization or a new member to this collective group. Someone just joining for the first time or even colleagues who have known each other for years and just didn't know the personal problems they were going through at work – it can be shocking.

How the group responds after that is important to group cohesion and to people finding the value and worth of the group. It can be overwhelming, and it can really make the group closer because they see the value of it or it make people distance themselves from the group and say this is just asking for trouble. So I think that structure really needs to be thought about beforehand and it can be as simple as having someone with a background in helping groups work through all of these emotions. We were blessed to have natural leaders in the very beginning who were able to manage the group feelings.

Our group leaders were willing to put themselves out into the spotlight and be an example for everyone else. For example, our leaders were able to read the room and say some issue needed to be discussed more OR say, "I think we need to take a break and save this for another discussion, so that everyone can have the chance to process what's going on." So it's really about keeping the group together and not letting it either fall apart because people become too risk-averse and keeping people grounded and reminding us to not do anything rash now that you've let these emotions out.

Those were some of the very early things that I saw and there's no blueprint for this. I saw different ways of dealing with it and I couldn't go back and tell you there was a right or wrong way because we were such a new group. I imagine for some people this group concept was too risky, or too different, or it lacked a concrete process that we are all accustomed to.

Personally, this entire experience was training myself to sit back, listen, and acknowledge people's experiences. I had to remind myself at the end of the day that I was hearing years' worth of pent-up or silenced emotions. Hearing peoples' stories all in one day or hearing this all in a few meetings was overwhelming. I had to remind myself that my experience might be different because I was so new. Because a lot of things for me were really positive at the time, right?

I just got a job. I have benefits for the first time. I have this, that and the other. But really reminding yourself about the positive things that the organization already does and not losing sight that this is a good place to work. We have the opportunity to have these discussions whereas in other places, these opportunities just don't exist. So within those very emotionally-charged conversations, having that space to remind yourself—as a whole— why are we doing this? It's to get better. It's to uncover the problem areas. How can we attempt to address them?

Especially now, when we have new members join our group, at the end of the meetings, in a kind of light-hearted fashion, I remind everyone "I know you're hearing a lot of negativity, but trust me, we're a fun group. We like each other. We generally find this a great place to work."

So in a nutshell, that is the risk you run: turning people very pessimistic because you are highlighting all of the uncovered issues.

Michelle: One of the things that I've discussed in my group with other consultants and other people who do this work, especially as it relates to affinity groups, is related to accountability. As in, how do we hold each other accountable as a group? For example, in situations where you have a member who may be doing something or behaving in a way that flies in the face of what the group is about or could cast a negative light on the group.

What are your thoughts about how to approach someone who is doing things that may bring harm to the perception or the organization, which ultimately affects us all?

CM: In the past, there have been instances where someone may have been doing something that's contrary to what the group believes or stands for. However, before that, before it got to any kind of problematic situation, that person reached out. I think as a group, you have to be aware that you are creating connections and someone is going to call you or email you share something with you.

You will be in a position to try and guide them or give them your opinion. As a group, we need more training on how to handle those situations. When someone says, "Hey, [x situation] is happening. I don't know what to do," or "I feel overwhelmed," we would serve ourselves better to get training on these situations. Ultimately, you can't control what someone does.

It's teaching each individual in your group how to respond or how to process that situation or what can be done in those scenarios before it escalates into consequences.

Those are proactive approaches. After that, I think there has to be a procedure or protocol. Something will inevitably happen and groups need a process to rely on that offers predictability. How do we get together and reach out to whoever might be involved and what the best approach will be?

I think one of those things is already built into these affinity groups. It's just getting together and checking in and saying, "How is everyone doing?" or "Is there something bothering people?" and people will have a chance to say, "Hey, I have something going on. I want to present it to the group and I don't know how to handle the situation," or, "I have something going on, but I really am sensitive about it. But I would like to talk with a few people on a private level right now."

I think that's what these affinity groups can do very well but everyone has to have buy-in and everyone has to feel like they're supported.

Michelle: So there are people that will read this book and they will be thinking about moving forward with an affinity group. What are some things that you would tell them to prepare for? Obviously every organization is different. But just based on your own personal experience, what are some things that you can say?

CM: New members. It seems obvious but it's something that can be easily forgotten about or pushed to the side or just not done entirely. You're going to have this group. You're going to be working on a bunch of different things, whether it's dealing with some issue or trying to write your own internal procedures or just trying to have a meeting together and your organization is going to continue with its normal everyday things.

People go on vacation. New people come in. People are hired. People leave and how you bring someone brand new up to speed is going to be critical to your group's future success, cohesion.

In any given point in time, there can be so much turnover and having something in place that attempts to educate anyone on your group's core values, why you were created, and what it is you're trying to do, and what is the vision that you have. That's important and it has to be memorialized in some way.

Otherwise, you will end up with this group who just doesn't have a lot of guidance. They kind of know that they meet every now and again – but what is it that they actually do?

What are the things that make it legitimate? Because you are taking time out of your workday. You are postponing other things to attend these meetings and like anything, it's easy to feel like this group just gets together, there's no direction, there's no concrete thing that's trying to be accomplished. Why am I going to spend my time doing that?

For example, why are you "checking in" at the beginning? That question can be so easy to miss because you can go around the room and just say, "How is everyone doing?" without knowing why you're asking that question, right?

And everyone can go around just saying, "Oh, I'm OK. I'm OK. I'm OK. I'm OK." Right? But the purpose, what is the fundamental purpose? Why are you checking in with everyone? This is why the group was created, to bring about any underlying issue that you're too hesitant to bring up elsewhere and creating the safe space to bring it up. And this is the chance, right?

But someone who doesn't know the purpose behind it can easily just ask, "How is everyone doing? OK? OK? Good." Next thing. So for me and any kind of tips and tricks that I've learned along the way, it's that – make sure that there's something or there's some way to bring in someone completely new and get them to understand why.

Michelle: What has CLS as an organization done well to support The Collective?

CM: Very basic: CLS has done well just by providing this opportunity and recognizing that this has to be done within the normal working hours. Just creating that space and opportunity was huge because if you're going to try and tell someone, "Hey, we're going to try and start this group," it's going to start either an hour before the workday starts or an hour after the workday ends. You're going to come across people who for a variety of different reasons can't. Whether it's family duties or other obligations that come up. Maybe they hold down another part-time job somewhere. If you really want to put your support behind the idea of these affinity groups, you have to do it on your own work time.

When an organization says "Yes, I support these groups and yes, you can meet during the normal business hours." You're recognizing that this is something that needs to be invested in.

Michelle: Any closing thoughts about The Collective, moving forward, what your hopes are, or anything at all? Or any thoughts about affinity spaces for people of color?

CM: There has to be so much buy-in to this group.

You can have this group and call it what you want in other organizations. But if people aren't committed to whatever the goal might be or whatever the vision might be, then that group is just going to exist on paper.

The group necessarily has to grow organically. But along the way, someone has to step back and look at the positives and negatives and keep an eye on cementing your group as something within the organization.

It's not just this random assortment of people who get together. Maybe in the beginning it has to be that. But as you grow, as you progress, you have to start putting in other systems in place or other procedures and memorializing things. For us, now, we have agenda. We have assigned group leaders. Every single one of our agendas has what we call reminders, which is a list of our group leaders' duties, what the note-takers' duties are, and what everyone else's duties are during the meeting.

Before, when we didn't have the agenda, people would wait for someone to take the lead on the meeting and the meetings would sometimes be a little too abstract. So, we designed our own internal processes. Someone was assigned to lead the meetings. And shortly after that, people were assigned to develop an agenda. That has really helped going forward, and our meetings aren't so scattered. They have a purpose, everyone is aware of it and there's always that room for someone to bring up something new. I hope we can just keep building off of that.

When issues come by, you need to step back and look at how it could have been handled better. What are we missing? What would have been great to have? "Did we miss an opportunity? How can we correct that later?" or "Did we give up something?" or "Does this make us look not unified?" Just constantly questioning what's going on so that the group as a whole can continue to go forward.

[End of Interview]

The White Allies Group

White staff members of CLS created a space where they could acknowledge and discuss their own racial identity and talk candidly about race as it specifically impacted their relationships with the CLS program, colleagues, clients, and cases/projects/campaigns. They were committed to being introspective and reflecting as individuals how to work as a group to fight racism at CLS and beyond.

The Purpose of the White Allies Group was:

1. To recognize/unpack how we, through the unearned privilege and power we have as white members of this society, encourage, help, or otherwise perpetuate race inequity in our relationships/work with our CLS (and other) colleagues and our clients and the harm that this causes; and,
2. To continue to change ourselves and our actions to reverse our course of inequity towards one of equity and justice.

One of the fundamental differences between white caucusing space and POC caucusing space, is that people of color have shared lived experiences as a result of simply **not being white**. So there will always be a common ground for all people of color to connect on. In general, people of color long for a space to belong.

For white people, whose belongingness is inherent, they come to this work without having a common ground. They have varying reasons for engaging in a caucus group, the challenge for white caucus groups is figuring out the group structure that will satisfy everyone's personal motivations. This seems to be one of the problems with many white caucus groups. While CLS was no different in that way, the white allies group was relentless in their commitment to find the right solution for the group.

Admittedly, this was one of my biggest surprises that I experienced at CLS. I spoke to each and every white ally group member to some degree about our race equity work throughout this process. Most of them demonstrated a very strong commitment to the work. Many of them stated they had a commitment to doing it. They ALL held very strong opinions and were absolutely keen on the issues of our state, region and country as it relates to race. I never *ever* considered that they couldn't openly share amongst themselves.

What is internalized racist superiority and how does caucusing help?

Crossroads defines internalized racist superiority as *"a complex multi-generational socialization process that teaches White people to believe, accept, and/or live out superior societal definitions of self and to fit into and live out superior societal roles. These Behaviors define and normalize the race construct and its outcome: white supremacy."*

White people are afforded the privilege of not having to be concerned about what life is like for people of color. Whereas, people of color, from a young age, are trained to know what the norms, rules (stated or unstated), expectations, likes/dislikes and concerns are for white people. This puts white people who are committed to anti-racism work, in the position of having to re-learn some things, and newly learn other things about the deep-seated issue of race. But more importantly, white people need to do this work *together* and without the additional burden being placed on people of color to educate them or "process" along with them. This is the main reason for white caucusing spaces.

Learning from other white people who are at different levels of understanding, pulling from the multitudes of available research articles, videos and anti-racist curriculums, give white people more than enough information to begin the work of confronting and addressing their internalized superiority as a group.

I am not saying that there isn't a need to have cross-racial dialogue and experiences. At CLS we intentionally incorporated mechanisms (trainings, articles, informal discussion groups, etc.) that provoked rich dialogue cross-racially, which continually strengthened our anti-racist work and vision. I am, however, saying that unpacking the effects of internalized superiority can re-traumatize folks of color who are constantly at the effect of it. Again, this is best done within white only spaces.

Internalized superiority at play

Following are some actual examples of internalized superiority at play. Again, they are a compilation of stories shared by other practitioners in this work as well as my own reflections.

- **Speaking up on behalf of people of color without input from people of color** –This is a common mistake. I think in an effort to "do something" during times of organizational flux, there is a need to act on behalf of a group who has not asked for it. This not only assumes that people of color can't advocate for themselves, but it assumes that white people know what they want or need. Let me be clear, this is different than seeing two black men getting thrown out of Starbucks and choosing to speak up as an ally. In those cases, I believe you absolutely should say something. We are talking at the organizational level.
- **Getting defensive** – We are all learning. This work requires a great deal of maturity, courage and humility. Mostly humility. We should all walk into this work 100% certain that we are going to do some things wrong. Some things we'll do very wrong. Some people will be offended. The worst thing

I've seen people do is get defensive or angry because they "didn't mean it that way". Or, they accuse the other person of being too sensitive. Some of the strongest, most active white allies I've seen have made some considerable mistakes, but have taken their lumps with grace and humility, which is a testament to their commitment to the work. This leads me to a final point about defensiveness and internalized superiority. If a mistake is made, don't disappear, or choose the "I'll never participate again" route. If we walk into this work expecting to fall on our face sometimes, the impact won't be as devastating.

- **Competing for the most "woke" award** – I was recently at a conference with about 300 people in attendance. There were two white women in particular who kept correcting others or calling them out – or as they say, "calling them in". For example, one of the panelists used the term, "differently-abled" and one of the women corrected them by saying that "People in the disabled movement don't like that term, and actually prefer the term 'disabled'". These kind of corrections by these women continued over the course of the two days. I also noticed that they were only correcting other white people. Finally, I overheard one woman say to the other, "I really thought that with an African American woman hosting this training, the panelists would have been more woke." I'm not sure what it's all about, but there is this trend in which some white people who are advocates for the work of race equity, start to beat up on other white people by over policing their language, judging their level of 'wokeness', and eventually creating an environment that is miserable for other white people to feel open and willing to share themselves--which is the entire point of caucusing. I would say to any white person who feels they are more woke than another white person, resist the urge of letting anyone know how woke you are, instead do two things. First, show your wokeness with your actions by making a difference. I mean, what's the sense of being woke if the world isn't a better place for it? Secondly, remember that in the grand scheme of this race equity work, we all know very little and there is so much for you (and us all) to learn.

- **Giving up** – Race work can be frustrating and it's easy to succumb to fatigue that comes along with it. Plus, when you look around at what's going on in our country it seems futile to even try climb this mountain. But one thing we know is that people of color can't *just take a break* from dealing with racism. The work of allyship means being there for the long haul. Without white people joining in on this fight, it surely won't end. This is the same at the organization level. If white caucus groups just said, "We can't get a structure in place, or we can't align our calendars, or some people are dominating the space, so we'll just not participate in the race conversation at this organization" that would be an epic mistake that demonstrated a stronger commitment to the racist structures we are working hard to challenge.

Looking back on the white allies' group, I struggled with the dilemma of jumping in and offering support, and allowing them space to do their own work. I felt like I had a vantage point that may offer a different perspective. But, they needed to go through their process and quite frankly, I think there was some resentment by some white allies who felt they were viewed as "broken" because they were not functioning in the same way that The Collective was. In speaking with my colleagues about white affinity spaces, our shared stories seem to indicate that this is a common experience of white ally groups. Finding their purpose and rhythm seems to take a little longer. I think it's different from group to group. Size matters, the composition matters, and the degree of fluency of race equity among team members' matters. There is no one size fits all approach.

There are many schools of thought about white affinity groups. For example, some think that not gelling as a group, or being mired in the process is just another form of detouring from the substantive race equity work. Others think that it's part of the process. Some feel that white ally groups are essential to the organizational healing process, and others think that they are a bad idea altogether. My position is that change can't happen without white people who are actively doing the internal work and reflection; and the issues that the white allies group at CLS experienced are no different than many, if not most white affinity group spaces who are doing real race equity work.

An Interview with a White Ally

Michelle: There are a lot of people who are considering implementing white ally groups and deciding whether or not they are a good idea. So, I thought it would be important to hear the voice of someone who's participating in a white affinity group.

So can you just give your overall experience of being in a white ally group in general?

W.A.: So I would say in general, I have found the experience somewhat frustrating. I don't want to say that that makes it not worthwhile. But it seems like white people tend to have a variety of perceptions of where we are in terms of being a dominant racial group in this country, and a different set of tools for dealing with that. And that variation makes it very hard to have everyone working in the same way on the same things at the same time.

If you add that to the fact that when you're white and the system works for you, you not only don't see issues sometimes, but also you don't feel driven in the same way to fix things or make corrections. There's not an urgency to it like it is if you are suffering from the oppressive side of that. That's not because you necessarily want to enjoy those things, but because it feels natural to have them.

So getting people together and on the same page and thinking about the same thing at the same time is more of a struggle. People don't always prioritize coming to the meetings. They spend a lot of time arguing about what to discuss and what's the best way to do things and some people who have been working at it longer and have more tools want to do things one way and other people don't see why you should do things that way.

So it's a little bit frustrating at times because I think it would be easier to let things slide and just enjoy the privileges of one's position in society. I think it's important to have for the sake of personal discipline, an obligation to participate in a group and be there and make that commitment because without it, no matter how great your intentions are, you tend to think about it when prompted by guilt as opposed to being actively connected with change.

Michelle: You mentioned urgency. As a white person, you don't necessarily have the same urgency that people of color do. What motivates your urgency for this dialogue?

W.A.: Well, I think it's a couple of things. I mean specifically related to the white affinity group that's formed here at CLS. I'm in a position where more of my colleagues I think are people of color than not, or at least were for a while.

I guess I'm privy to information or experiences that makes me feel an affinity for my legal assistant/ paralegal group, and I feel some solidarity there. So I think in some ways that keeps me connected to hear other people's stories and say, "Hey, wait a minute. That hasn't happened to me. That's not a positional problem. That's a race problem, and by the way, that makes me angry because you and I are the same."

So in some ways, that has been helpful to me to have those conversations. Then also that has driven me to spend a lot of time researching racism and privilege and intersectionality and the more I read and the more I participate in my personal life with other groups, the more that drives me to say, "Hey, it's important that we keep doing this and it's important to keep driving it."

There have been some times in the white ally formation or the white affinity group formation where I've just been like, "Oh, I don't want to do this anymore. I'm so tired of it."

Then I think about a couple of things. One is when Dr. Leticia Nieto said in one of our trainings that when you are part of the dominant culture, whatever it is, whether it's cisgender identification or being white or being male or whatever, when you are wanting to actively engage in ally ship, one of your jobs is to bring along or to provide more tools to people in your same group that haven't got there yet or aren't there with you, so that's one thing I think about.

Then the other thing I think about is how people of color don't have that option. Well, I mean they can get tired but they don't get to be tired and just ignore it because it's there all the time.

So when I get tired and I say I don't feel like doing this anymore, these people should just figure it out for themselves. They're not whatever – that I say to myself. If other people don't have a choice, then I don't get to make that choice.

That's kind of me – I mean one of the things that drive my urgency is me trying to hold myself responsible for not being complicit.

Michelle: So you said a little earlier about white people having a variation on their perspective, their tools and their readiness to engage in this conversation. This brings up this idea that I've noticed more and more and that is the idea of 'wokeness' and what it means to be 'woke'. Can you give me your thoughts about this idea of being woke?

W.A.: I think that sort of comes out of a cultural expectation of "rightness." That if I'm not right, I'm wrong. There's this really bifurcated view of how things are. I don't like to use the word "woke" because I feel like that's culturally appropriated from a different perspective. So I don't really like that from the origins of the word "woke" to its adoption and to white sort of liberal culture. I'm not keen on that phrase at all.

But I think it's very deeply embedded in us like Robin DiAngelo said, "racism is bad", and it *is* bad to be *actively in pursuit of racism* - but racism is something that we've had fed into us and that we're unconsciously taking in – from the second we become conscious that there's other people out there.

So there's nothing – there's no way you can purge yourself of that completely, but you can be more aware of where you are and work on challenging one's own assumptions, et cetera. But part of that is this – "well, if I'm racist, then I'm bad" - so I *need* to be less-racist so I can be "good." I need to be right. I need to be righter than the next guy and everything starts to become a competition. And the best thing that I got out of our last training with *Dr. Nieto* is this – I don't need to be right. In fact if I'm right all the time, I'm not learning because I'm so busy defending my rightness that I can't get anywhere.

So I think it would help us all to be able to internalize that and stop worrying about it. But I do think that it can be damaging in a group to have leadership or a subset of people within the group who will then turn around and jump on somebody who's maybe not spent as much time thinking about or engaged in anti-oppression work within themselves, and who using the tools that they have as a means of turning around and re-oppressing somebody else. That's not helpful.

Actually I would say to our credit, my experience in the white allies group so far has not looked like that to me. So we've got that going for us, which is nice.

Michelle: So you've actually been in two different white ally group experiences. Can you share about your experience in those two groups?

If there was somebody that came to you and said, "Hey, we're think-ing about creating a white ally group at our organization. What are some of the good things that have come from both groups?" What are some of the things that you would say that absolutely do not work?

W.A.: So first we had a meeting with everybody present and some of the people who were facilitating that meeting, which was not me at the time, had done some research and had read that affinity groups worked better if they have ideally five to ten members. We were about 18 to 20 people at the time.

So it seemed to make sense to make two smaller groups because we didn't know what we were doing. We just read something because, you know, white people like to have a recipe for success. Then we said, well, if we just break into two groups, that's the right thing to do. We've read it some place. It's what we're advised to do and so we did.

The two groups didn't really have communication with each other or leadership that was working in concert. People self-selected into the groups based on the times they were meeting and so one of the groups had two members that had done extensive work before in various anti-oppression groups, affinity-based, anti-oppression groups and they had suggestions and that was the group that I fell into based on meeting time.

The other group didn't really have anyone with experience to sort of take charge or to start facilitating and saying, "Hey, here are some things that I've done before. Do we want to try any of these?"

I don't know what went on in those meetings. But I heard that they struggled quite a bit with what their purpose was and what they should be doing and that virtually every meeting they had turned into this discussion of what they should do and what their purpose was.

The group that I went into, I said at the first meeting that I felt very strongly that we should not be engaging in organizational change type activity. That is, we shouldn't be determining, "oh, here are problems and we should solve them". I felt very uncomfortable in a group of white people making decisions like that because I felt like that perpetuated a racist structure that we wouldn't have necessarily the self-knowledge to know if what we were suggesting was helpful. I felt we should just be focused on our own internal anti-oppression work, and reading about white privilege and where we fit into that, and talking about what aspects of that culture we see in our workplace and what we personally reinforce.

We met pretty much monthly and we kind of rotated leadership and we had a question to introduce what we were talking about that day. We were just kind of cooking along and then The Collective put out a letter to CLS outlining problems that they had seen and suggesting institutional changes to correct those problems and a way to sort of bring everybody together and to the one CLS. So that was the introduction of that concept.

The other white group which had been struggling to find its purpose said, "Ah-ha! We know what to do. Change. We got to do the change. We need to respond and we need to get on the horse with the sword out and go. *This* is what we do!" And my group was like, "Hey, hey, hey. We're only white people. We're not really sure if that's what our purpose as a group is."

So during that process, I came to the conclusion that a white affinity group in any kind of institutional setting should be very clear about what their purpose is at the beginning of gathering. In my opinion, I feel like the most important thing to know is that you're not the other side of the coin of whatever affinity groups have formed for people of color or if you're doing along gender lines or whatever.

When you're the agent group, your purpose is not to do whatever the other group is doing necessarily. You may need to support their work. You may need to provide some administrative support. So for instance if they say we need to form committees to look for this, we say, "Hey, we've got six members who want to serve on those committees and here they are. We're producing them to support your work." That kind of support may be necessary.

But your job is not to do the same thing they're doing. You're not looking at the same issues. You're not coming from the same place or the same culture. To work harmoniously with that other group, you do need to do some of that internal work or recognition work and giving everyone the same tools and the same knowledge, so that you're ready to support the other affinity group when they want to make change.

That's just my opinion of what the purpose of a white affinity group should be based on my experience. But I don't know. That's where I am.

Michelle: So one group was looking more at solutions and when the Collective letter came out, they had something to react to which became the driving force to some extent. Whereas your group was more introspective and now you had something to react to, to go deeper into the work that you were doing on yourself and how you were complicit in the issues that were raised in The Collective.

W.A.: Correct.

Michelle: I also understand that the group that was more introspective and reflective that you said seemed to work pretty well were all women and the other, more solution-oriented group, were predominantly men with women weaving in and out of the group. Do you think that the different approaches to this work (and the Collective Letter) had anything to do with gender—without generalizing about men?

W.A.: I definitely think that played a part and I think really because being in a group with all women, it's hard for me to say because now I'm speaking from a woman versus man perspective. So how I feel being a woman probably affects how I think men behave. But I feel like men don't often want to go personal and if white people have a need to be right, I feel like white men have an even greater need to be right because culturally and historically and Christianically I guess, the man is in charge, the man is blah, blah, blah. The man makes the decisions. The man rules society.

So I guess with that comes a certain responsibility to be right or do it right or have things be right all the time. That includes not admitting to weakness or personal weakness.

Michelle: Or vulnerability.

W.A.: Yeah. Women – and especially women in a group with just women tend to be more vulnerable and sometimes are willing to talk about experiences. You can almost have like in some ways – it's not the same kind of oppression but an oppression reference point at least.

You can say, yeah, I remember when a guy did this and I was like – I wasn't even sure if I was being insulted or not. I can imagine what that felt like for this other person who said that they weren't sure if this white person meant to insult them or not.

There's a bridge I guess to that experience or to being able to empathize with that experience. So I think being able to empathize with somebody else's experience of oppression makes it in some ways easier to access your own ability to engage in that oppression. I don't know.

I do think it played a role and I think just the comfort of not having somebody talk over me ever, or the group was very focused around consensus and having a consensus-based decision-making system. So are we done with this topic? Everybody had to agree we were done with the topic before we could move on whereas – as soon as we rein-tegrated the two groups, we no longer had a consensus-based system. I feel like the male members of the group did not have patience for that and also the group was pretty large. So bringing a group that large to consensus is difficult. We wound up doing everything by majority vote. So very different vibe.

Michelle: Got it. It really makes me think about the different ways that you can approach this work and one of the things that you said pretty consistently about what works is to get into these smaller groups. I mean best practices say that's the way as well.

W.A.: Yeah. I mean going back to breaking into two groups and then not having any kind of co-facilitatorship for those two groups, that was a huge mistake because then the two groups were completely cast to their own devices to figure out what they should be doing and that led to this perception that nobody knew what was happening.

I mean even if you had two groups and you met quarterly as a large group to talk about what you've been doing and you had the co-facilitator's meeting monthly before those meetings, to make sure everybody is on the same trajectory, that would be good.

It just doesn't work to give people an open forum for discussion with-out direction. I gather that's very different from how things worked well in The Collective.

That's partially because no group of white people is going to get together and say, "Hey, I oppressed someone today. I feel really bad about it. How can I do that differently next time?"

Maybe one day we will be that driven and that good. But we're not even close to there yet.

Michelle: Right.

W.A.: So, having a structure and a set of expectations is very important when you're forming an affinity group.

There's always some voices in the room that say, hey, we just gotta get working. We can't stop to worry about whether or not we're doing this the right way. Seriously, I can't tell you how many times people said that. But are we doing this the right way? Is there another model we can use? What can we base ourselves off of?

I don't know. I'm just going to give you an example from my life. So one time I put a down pillow in the drier and a ticking broke on it. When I opened up the drier, I mean you've never seen such a mess in your life.

Like all the feathers came flying out of the drier and there was a big pile of feathers in the drier. I mean it was a mess. I just started laughing because I was like, "Oh my god, this mess is so huge. I don't even know where to start."

I feel like when you put a bunch of white people in the room and say, "Start working on your anti-oppression, anti-racism," everybody is like, "There are so many feathers!"

So, I just get a broom and I start sweeping and the feathers are flying. I'm not getting anywhere. Eventually my husband came down to see what the heck was going on down there and he brought me a Shop-Vac and that was very useful. But still for like weeks, still I would occasionally find a feather in my laundry room.

So, I think the knowledge that there's like not really a right way to start and you may stumble on the right tool, that works for you for a while. But even then, it's not going to fix the problem. You're still going to be finding feathers everywhere.

If you get the right tool, what you might have is a group of people who have this same set of tools and are on the same page. You know, with the same amount of dedication. But you're not going to get there.

Michelle: So, do you think that the approach should be for people to go into this work saying, "Hey, listen. There will be feathers. There will be feathers *everywhere*,"? Or is the approach to go in with a Shop-Vac and prepare everyone for the massive feathering that will take place? Which one do you think is the most supportive and the most sustainable approach to doing this work?

W.A.: I think that's a false dichotomy there, Michelle. I think you go into it saying this is the best tool we have that we're aware of *and* there's going to be feathers. We're going to start out using this tool and hey, if we discover another one, fantastic. We're going to use that one too. It's our responsibility to keep looking for more tools. But there's going to be feathers and if we wait for the guarantee that all feathers will be taken care of, we are going to fail. We're going to stand and staring at a pile of feathers. So, I have another analogy I use that involves a pile of sand.

I say, OK, so I got a spoon. I'm going to start with a spoon. If I happen to locate a shovel, great. I'm going to get the shovel. But chances are I'm never going to reach the bottom and get all the grains of sand gathered up. That doesn't mean it's not worth moving.

So I think what doesn't work is to have an expectation that you're going to come in. You're going to do the thing and then you're going to be done with the thing.

You're not going to be done. You're not going to be right. Sometimes you're going to be wrong and you're going to do the wrong things or you're going to say the wrong things. Sometimes The Collective is going to come to you, or whatever the other affinity group is, will come to you and say, "Hey, we think you're doing the wrong thing," and you should listen to that.

I think it's important for the affinity groups to check in with each other and to know what each other are working on. So that The Collective group doesn't think you are a secret white cabal of people deciding how things are going to be.

Michelle: I mentioned this concept of internalized superiority which is defined by an organization called Crossroads as a condition in which white people accept, believe and live out notions of superiority above all other races. In the white allies group, did you observe any attitudes or actions that you believed were a result of internalized superiority?

W.A.: I would say that internalized white superiority supports our feeling that the privileges of our race are human rights. So, when we go to base the expectations of the group and group discussion, a lot of those "rights" get expressed right there. A right to safety/security, a right to speak, a right to feel like one's thoughts are welcome, a right to feel comfortable in a room, a right to feel right. We tend to make rules and expectations within our affinity groups that enforce these things we understand intrinsically as our "rights", but are really expectations we have of any social or group situation, as a result of a lifetime of whiteness. We find it shocking when we discover our colleagues (or family members, or friends of color) don't feel that same comfort, welcomeness, etc. as a right of existing. And instead of challenging whether or not those are rights or appropriate expectations, we soldier on trying to reinforce them, and think up systems whereby our colleagues of color will be able to operate under that same system of privileges. Our general idea of anti-oppression work tends towards unilaterally deciding that desirable social change extends the rights of whiteness *over* people of color. But it never really challenges the rights of whiteness. I don't know how to address this in an affinity group. But I sure see it play out there.

On that basis, I can say yes, I definitely see there are times and I felt times in the larger discussion when there's somebody who's male, who disagrees with me and sometimes I would rather just stop talking than discuss it any further. I could feel that it's like that.

OK. I'm just going to accept this, that they're going to talk over me and I'm not going to fight about it. So I mean I could feel that kind of thing go on. But I don't know that I have enough tools to know when it's happening on a race basis.

Michelle: So there's going to be people who approach this work. People are going to read this book and they're going to say, "You know what? I really want to do it," or there may those that say, "I think not – I'm not equipped for feathers." Having been going through this now for a couple of years, what would you say that people should be prepared for when joining a white allies' group?

W.A.: I would they should be prepared for the fact that many people are going to argue about what it is you should be doing and what your purpose is. That kind of detouring will happen pretty regularly, particularly when anyone gets really uncomfortable on a personal level with what's being discussed.

There will be retreat and there will be then this sort of retreat to a global existential conversation. I don't know why we do it but that's what we seem to do.

The thing that I wasn't fully prepared for or that I think people should be prepared for is that people bring their personal lives and experiences to the group and those lives and experiences can include things like spouses or partners, children of color, adopted children of color. I would say that I've seen sometimes people aren't able, from the closeness of their family members, really look at certain issues either because it's too painful to think that their family member might be experiencing that or it's too painful for them to think that they might be engaged in oppression with regards to those family members.

So sometimes the conversation can go off topic where people won't want to delve in too far because for instance they know their colleague has two adopted children of color and they don't want to talk about adoption or foster care in terms of how social oppression drives adoption of children of color.

So that I wasn't prepared for those kinds of things and I didn't really understand how that was going to work until I was in the middle of a discussion and found myself censoring myself.

Michelle: Any closing thoughts?

W.A.: I would say I'm very grateful for having had the very frustrating experience of doing this and hope to continue to frustrate myself for some time because I do think it's worthwhile and it has been worthwhile on a personal level, from encouraging myself to look deeper, to dig deeper, to look at what I'm doing in my life and at my work.

I think one of the things that stuck with me from Robin DiAngelo is to say that when you're in a position of privilege, you don't necessarily see it. I mean, people talk about it from the position of privileges that you enjoy or whatever. But you don't see that those are also a loss, and all the things you lose by sitting in that position because you didn't gain the full participation of your colleague.

I feel like it has encouraged me to think about what it is that I lose every day as a result of institutionalized oppression.

Finally, I'm aware of the concept of white privilege, the privilege to feel "comfortable" or "safe" in race-based discussions and that can be considered one reason why white affinity groups shouldn't exist. I rejected that reasoning, because I think it may sometimes be necessary to use that if the result is that the we expand our consciousness and anti-oppression toolbox. If we think of affinity groups as one of a number of tools we are using to break institutional racism/oppression, then I think of this as one tool. As with all tools, one should use it thoughtfully and intentionally, and not just default to it out of comfort.

[End of Interview]

b. Agreements and Values

Your organization's culture is driven by the values and agreements of the people. After working with different organizations I wholeheartedly believe that not only is it important to understand the organizational agreements and values, but it is equally important to understand how they inform the day-to-day interactions and operations. Because of this, defining organizational agreements and values should be an absolute priority for the leader, and needs to be consistently communicated, reinforced *and modeled* by leadership.

I was part of the Office Culture team. We really struggled with the concept of "culture" and how to approach it. How do we define our organizational culture? How do we transform something that we struggled to define? We eventually narrowed the concept of culture down to a working definition – something along the lines of "the values, agreements and beliefs that guide our behavior at CLS". With this definition it became a glaring reality that while we had a clear commitment related to our clients, we had no shared values/agreements about how we would treat each other. So, we began by approaching the concepts of "agreements" and "values" as two separate things. **Agreements** addressed our *behavior and treatment* of one another, **values** are the *underlying motivations* that inform and guide our behavior.

Agreements

We first established our agreements. Following is the process used to narrow down to CLS's current five agreements.

Let's rewind back to May 2017 at our #OneCLS Day retreat. During this retreat, we did an exercise in which we broke up into groups and reflected on the following questions:

- What would it be like to bring your full self to work?
- What do you need to be able to be your full self at work?

Each group had a note taker who would report out to the entire group what their group had discussed. At the end of the day, I collected all the notes from each note taker and entered the raw data into a word document. Moving through this like a research project, I took all of the raw data from the group discussion and began to pull out common words and themes to be able to identify some shared values. Sure enough, you could see similarities in what people cared about and what they felt was missing in order for them to feel safe enough to bring their full self to work.

Now, with this raw data, the Office Culture team was able to come up with six agreements that they felt captured what staff had valued and said they needed. We would then propose these six agreements to all staff at our next staff retreat only a few months away.

At the staff retreat, we broke into groups and discussed the values. After an hour, all staff actually ended up agreeing on four of six of the values which was pretty miraculous. The fifth agreement needed some re-tooling, so I worked on that one with staff over email and Survey Monkey for the next month or so until we finally got it right. The sixth agreement we tossed all together. For those of you curious folks, the sixth agreement was, "*We choose to be transparent by sharing our assumptions and intentions.*" At the time, many staff didn't feel they could be transparent, and hierarchical differences brought into question whether or not any one would really ever be fully transparent with their supervisor. It felt like too much of a stretch and so we scrapped it. Here are the five agreements we landed on:

1. We choose to be conscious of our differences and the uniqueness of others
2. We choose to be accountable for our impact
3. We choose to listen with kindness and compassion
4. We choose to communicate with respect
5. We seek to understand before rushing to judgment

There are a couple of things to notice. The first thing was that we deliberated about the phrase "we choose". We designed these agreements to be accessible. We know that being accountable for our impact is a choice, or being respectful when communicating is a choice. Even when we were discussing them, one of the team members said, "we want agreements that you can activate." For example, when you are in a meeting and someone is taking up a lot of space, or being rude, you can say to yourself, "I'm really triggered right now, but I'm going to *choose to communicate with respect*". Let's say you miss the mark and get really snarky with that co-worker, you can then *choose to be accountable for your impact* and clean things up.

The second thing you'll notice is that the fifth agreement begins with we "seek" rather than "choose". This is because staff felt that seeking to understand was more authentic. Sometimes one's understanding of something doesn't really feel like a choice, but *seeking* to understand is not only a choice, but it's an ongoing process, and felt more natural and authentic.

Values

A year after establishing our agreements of our behavior toward one another, we were now ready to create our values. Our leadership team felt it was important to understand those values *or motivations* that drive our behavior not only toward each other, but in the communities we serve.

Similar to the agreements process, here is the process we underwent to establish our values:

1. First, we found one of those values' lists online. I will share the list in the resources section of this book. We gave that values' list to each staff member to choose their top eight values.
2. I gathered all lists from each staff member and created one master synthesized list. Thankfully, many of the values were shared by staff, so after duplicates, the values list was narrowed down to 87 different values held by all staff.
3. To whittle the values down more, I counted all values that got five or more votes by staff and tossed the rest. This took the total number of values down to 14 values.
4. I shared those 14 values with all staff and asked them to re-vote but this time only choose their top 4 of the 14 listed.
5. Again, only choosing those that got 5 or more votes, the following are the top 10 votes that were most important to staff.

   1. Compassion
   2. Accountability
   3. Making a difference
   4. Humor
   5. Collaboration
   6. Community
   7. Creativity
   8. Inclusiveness
   9. Humility
   10. Fairness

Working together as a group to determine our agreements and values may have been time consuming, but it was important to have input and buy-in from all staff. The work of equity is, after all, about establishing a culture that we all create and build together.

c. Relationship building

Building meaningful relationships at work is more important than a lot of people will admit. The social dynamics at work become even more essential when you are doing race equity work which is fraught with tension and discomfort. I can say that some of my coworkers at CLS were my friends and afforded me grace when I made mistakes... because they cared about me on a personal level.

Sure, there are studies about how work environments can have a negative or positive impact on one's health, or how it affects organizational productivity, but I found that the main benefit has been that I feel like I'm part of something meaningful with people that I enjoy being around.

That said, I think CLS was on the mark by investing time, energy, and resources in to finding ways to build relationships. Other than caucusing and creating shared agreements about how we would treat each other, we also did the following things to strengthen relationships.

- **CLS paid for caucus groups to meet once a year in person**. We had five different offices and met monthly on skype. However once a year, The Collective and White Ally Groups could meet in person with their fellow caucus mates. Many organizations wouldn't allocate resources for two groups to travel across the state to meet together specifically to talk about race. This was a significant commitment on CLS's end.
- **We had a monthly theme that we'd focus on**. On the first of the month, every staff member would get an email with the theme, an article and reflection questions. Ideally, staff would talk about it in their caucus groups. But we added a skype lunch session called, "Hungry for Equity" where we would

talk about the article across race and offices. We had our entire year's themes planned out. One time, two staff of color were entering the office and a white man walked up to them, pointed at them and said, "Hey look, a Black and a Mexican". More words were exchanged, but that isn't really important here. What is important is that it was pretty upsetting for these staff members and those of us who care about them. It was then that we decided to incorporate personal experiences as learning/growing opportunities as opposed to simply reading articles, or watching videos. So, that month's theme being "fear", we shared that story and posed the following questions:

o What would you do in that situation
o What would you do if you observed your coworkers in that situation?
o How do we best support each other during those situations?
o What are some of the fears that could/would have stopped you?

We wanted to provide opportunities for people to move beyond the abstract and have conversations based on real accounts of our staff's experiences.

- **We started to focus on more fun at staff retreats.** The last staff retreat I went to was at Sleeping Lady where people swam, hiked, sang karaoke, ate great food, played board games until the wee hours of the night, and played fun trivia games. We also had a guest speaker that pushed us to connect with the more vulnerable aspects of our humanity. Of course we still worked on moving our advocacy, strategic planning and organizational goals forward, but we made sure to have more fun along the way.
- **We created #OneCLS Day as an annual event.** In addition to being able to meet in person within caucuses, CLS also

created space for us to share and connect face to face about our race equity work, reflections, and progress as an entire organization.

At the end of the day, these are the kinds of experiences that make organizations stronger, more cohesive, and better able to serve and connect with clients.

2. Managing Conflict

The following is an excerpt from a 2008 report entitled, Workplace Conflict and How Businesses can Harness it to Thrive", produced by CPP Global.

"First and foremost, workers at all levels must learn to accept conflict as an inevitable part of their work environment – the study found that an over-whelming majority (85%) of employees at all levels experience conflict to some degree. Furthermore, we found that U.S. employees spend 2.8 hours per week dealing with conflict, equating to approximately $359 billion in paid hours in 2008. If managed improperly, businesses' productivity, operational effectiveness, and morale take a major hit, as evidenced in our finding that 27 percent of employees have witnessed conflict morph into a personal attack, while 25 percent say that the avoidance of conflict resulted in sickness or absence from work."

Conflict will always be present at the individual and organizational levels. While it may be unavoidable, it *is* manageable. I'll say that differently. It *must* be managed. The financial burden of neglecting conflict can be extremely heavy. For nonprofits who are often hyper-vigilant about every penny, it's even more taxing.

Some of the causes I've seen related to conflict include poor communication, lack of organizational values and agreements, personality differences, poor leadership skills, organizational changes and conflicts of interest. While racialized conflicts occur, they are often masked by one of the aforementioned causes.

Whatever the cause of the conflict, my experience is that it can be better managed by staff who are equipped with skills to honestly self reflect, and who have the capacity to more willingly accept others. While this can be done through a comprehensive conflict management training, it is reinforced by organizational values, agreements, social connections and *especially* modeling by leadership.

Our leadership team sought to find a way to innovatively manage conflict in a transformative way that moved us away from a reactive/punitive model to a proactive/restorative model where people were encouraged to self reflect and work together.

The Collective Letter stated that "CLS inconsistently addresses, or fails to address, concerns raised by staff of color regarding decision making, input, and staff dynamics." They went on to say that as result, staff of color are impacted in the following ways:

- Distrust and fear between all staff.
- No safe space to address concerns on race or other sensitive issues.
- General discomfort about issues of race as a conduit to ONE CLS.
- No opportunity for real transformational dialogue to occur between white and nonwhite staff as no one is speaking up.
- Academic discussion on race equity keeps the conversation of race at a cerebral/technical level requiring no personal reflection or change.

We were really committed to striking a balance between effectively responding to staff and their concerns, while normalizing conflict as a natural part of working together and being human. Therefore, we set out to find the best model to address the aforementioned issues and that also resonated with our five agreements.

a. Restorative Justice & Culture

During this time, which was a little over a year after The Collective Letter went out, Travis Andrews joined me in our race equity work. Travis had extensive experience with a concept called **Restorative Justice.** Merf had also mentioned Restorative Justice as a potential conflict management model and showed great enthusiasm for it, but until Travis came along we never moved forward with it because I wasn't knowledgeable enough to understand how it would work. But now, with Travis's experience and Merf's enthusiastic support, I began to look more deeply at how it could actually be an effective way for us to move from a model of conflict that focuses on punishment of individuals, rather than restoring them. I cross checked the Restorative Justice model with the five impacts that The Collective listed and felt confident that this model was right for our staff. After a couple of false starts, we introduced the concept of Restorative Justice to staff at #OneCLS Day 2018 and they liked the idea, so we adopted its guidelines on how we'd manage conflict. This process did not supersede our union grievance process that addresses more complex issues such as sexual harassment, discrimination, retaliation etc. This process serves as a guideline for our day-to-day interactions that involve, conflict or misunderstandings. The idea is that the more we use the process, the less likely issues will rise to the level of grievance.

What is Restorative Justice?

"Restorative Justice" describes a dialogue process of resolving conflict. Originally used in the criminal justice system, it related to severe crimes, and provided a platform for victims and offenders to engage in dialogue that promoted forgiveness, redemption and healing.

What is a Restorative Culture?

As Restorative Justice evolved, more and more organizations began to realize that they can use Restorative Justice Principles in their daily work to build, maintain and repair relationships. With this change in objective came a change in terminology - **Restorative Culture**. Columbia Legal Services has joined a long list of organizations who embrace the philosophy of a restorative culture as a means to address conflict, team-build and encourage honest dialogue aimed at creating a greater sense of community and safety.

Restorative Culture: Framing Conflict

PUNITIVE	RESTORATIVE
Narrower focus on a particular conflict and its resolution	Focuses on relationships and stronger work community
How has the organization been harmed/damaged?	Who/what relationships have been harmed /damaged?
Who is Guilty?	Who is the responsible party and what was needed? All parties included in dialogue/healing
Accountability = Guilt = Punishment	Accountability = Acknowledging impact and restoring those who have been affected
Focus on punishment, without opportunity to make amends	Offender is given opportunity to make amends or express remorse

CLS's restorative culture is made up of two components – **Formal Restorative Processes** and **Informal Restorative Practices**.

Formal Restorative Practices

Formal restorative practices are often used *reactively* to address conflict while informal restorative practices are typically used as a *proactive* measure to prevent harm. Here is a high-level overview of the process that CLS used.

1. Every attempt should be made to resolve the conflict or dispute *with that person directly.*

    a. If the staff member is uncomfortable speaking with the individual directly for any reason, then they can request the support of a Peer Resolution Advocate (PRA). The PRA will provide support to the reporting person and if appropriate can make contact with the other party to prompt discussion.

2. <u>Restorative conflict resolution is not mandatory.</u> If both parties agree to manage their conflict through Restorative Practices, they can choose from the following direct intervention options:

    a. One-on-one coaching/Mentoring around navigating conflict and difficult conversations.
    b. Restorative Mediation (Internal) – Both Parties agree to sit with the PRA with a clear intent of reflecting on the conflict and exploring different perspectives that will help in developing a plan to achieve resolution.
    c. Restorative Mediation (External) – Both parties agree to sit with an external facilitator with a clear intent of reflecting on the conflict and exploring different perspectives that will help in developing a plan to achieve resolution.

3. If resolution is not reached with the above intervention options, the parties should refer to the collective bargaining grievance process.

4. In some cases of longstanding or severe issues, there may be some collateral impact on teams/groups that have been witness to or indirectly involved in conflict. Parties may request, or agree to, a restorative circle which allows for broader group discussion, healing and restoration

Informal Restorative Practices

Informal restorative processes are used to build relationships within a group or community, to prevent or minimize the likelihood of conflict or harm occurring, rather than solely in response to an incident of harm. The use of informal restorative processes to maintain and strengthen relationships, and even build them where they do not currently exist, leads to safer and stronger communities where the incidence of harm occurring is reduced.

Key features:

- They are used by individuals integrated into their daily work, rather than as a discrete, separate process.
- Restorative skills are used on the spot to deal with conflict as it occurs, rather than after the event and following a time of preparation.
- Informal restorative processes can involve work with just one individual, with two people, or as a group process.

People instinctively do what is most comfortable and safest, which is triangulating conversations, avoiding, or engaging in passive aggressive behavior rather than summoning the courage and vulnerability to let another person know how they are feeling. Implementing the work of a restorative culture takes a long time as is it based on building relationships and trust. This work will require organizational patience and fortitude to ensure its success.

C. The Justice Work

When it comes to integrating race equity, this is the part that most organizations focus on – the structures, systems and technical aspects of the work. This is probably because it's easier to change a policy rather than a heart or mind. Nevertheless, it is still and important part of the work.

If you recall earlier, I mentioned that the "justice" or more technical work in the Collective letter was related to our **hiring practices** and **professional development**; and while we made many changes, I will highlight these two areas.

1. Hiring Practices

I appreciate the organizations who come to me with a desire to increase diversity within their organizations. Unfortunately, the only trick they have up their sleeve is to hire more people of color, which does nothing to ensure these new hires are welcomed, or that the culture is conducive for their success.

I can't stress enough the importance of *first* ensuring that your organization is prepared for new staff of color to do their best work. This is why focusing on the culture/social aspects of the organization is more important than changing the policies, practices or people. You'll just end up experiencing a high turnover rate of staff of color.

Having a diverse staff is absolutely important, yes. Above all they should be intentionally chosen with your mission and values squarely in mind. Also, as your mainline connection to your clients, your staff should be well equipped, supported and empowered to do their best work.

The Collective identified three areas of concern as it relates to our hiring and retention practices:

- CLS lacks a clear hiring process, which is a concern to many staff of color. Decision-making in the hiring process is often arbitrary and there is no formalized interview team with well-developed policies and hiring criteria. For example, staff members have been brought onto an interview panel at the last-minute, without sufficient time to review the applicant's materials or time to discuss questions and the criteria being used to evaluate the applicants.
- Additionally, The Collective is concerned that CLS lacks a formal and effective recruitment process.
- Finally, The Collective is concerned about integration and retention of new hires.

Travis and I went through this process in grueling detail to check for any areas that may need to be considered, or reconsidered. While we had a pretty solid process in place already, our primary aim was to make sure that we were using an equity baseline throughout the entire process. And even if we were, the issue was that it wasn't written down as such, which left room for confusion about how we craft job descriptions, who we reach out to, who is on the selection panel (and how their input is weighed) and how the new hire is set up for success once they come on board.

CLS hiring and recruitment

The strength and success of CLS' advocacy efforts require inclusion of people with unique ideas and perspectives and the insight gained from their experiences. CLS is committed to fostering a diverse workplace and inclusive environment.

CLS developed a comprehensive recruitment program to ensure the most diverse and skilled applicant pool. Following are the four essential phases to this program: job analysis/description, outreach and recruitment, interview and selection, and ongoing targeted outreach/relationship building.

Phase I – Job Analysis

Job duties and responsibilities often evolve over time, thus job descriptions need periodic review to ensure client and program needs' are met. Consequently, before posting any vacant positions a systematic procedure for gathering, documenting, and analyzing information about the content, context, and requirements of the position is necessary. This will help to identify the essential functions and the necessary competencies, knowledge, skills, and abilities required.

Purpose:

➢ To ensure that leadership reviews each new job opening as an opportunity to expand the program with new energy, fresh ideas and different approaches to the work, as opposed to "putting another butt in the seat".
➢ To allow for strategic, efficient and effective recruitment of diverse candidates by ensuring language in job description is inclusive and transparent.

Questions to Ask:

➢ Who has been involved in vetting the job description before it goes out?
➢ Have members of the team that will work with the new hire had an opportunity to give any input, formal or informal?
➢ Has someone seen the job description who has the fluency and astuteness to notice any potential equity red flags or concerns?

Phase II - Equitable Outreach and Recruitment

To optimize CLS's culture and to better engage the communities we serve, we must operate with a targeted outreach plan. The targeted outreach plan is the strategy we use to broaden our efforts and recruit to attract qualified diverse applicants. Through the engagement and creation of intentionally diverse relationships, we strive to equitably produce and recruit qualified applicants.

When posting externally, we focus on several factors: how far/wide we'd like to do a search (national search vs. targeted regional), increasing and encouraging the diversity of our applicant pool, and ensuring that it reaches intended, wide audiences.

Purpose:

> ➤ To promote a workforce that reflects the communities we serve, making us better advocates for our clients
> ➤ To enhance the overall culture and breadth of experience/knowledge to CLS

Questions to Ask:

> ➤ Do you/can you recruit internal staff for this position? (What are your organization's values related to grooming staff to grow into leadership positions?)
> ➤ Where are you posting the job description?
> ➤ Are you being intentional about posting at outlets that have a diverse audience?
> ➤ Are candidates required to provide an equity statement, and is it weighed appropriately in the evaluation of the candidate?

Phase III - Interviewing and Selection

CLS is committed to changing the way we engage within our hiring process. By being intentional and proactive in our interviews and selection process, we are able to look beyond a resume and gain a deeper understanding of what motivates an applicant and what has drawn them to our work. Simultaneously, we forge a relationship with our applicants that can motivate them to apply for future openings if they are not selected.

Purpose:

> ➢ To help staff confront and unpack biases that could arise during the interview and selection process
> ➢ To establish clear and consistent protocols and criteria to evaluate candidates

Questions to Ask:

> ➢ Do you/can you recruit internal staff for this position? (What are your organization's values related to grooming staff to grow into leadership positions?) If there are internal applicants, are they interviewing along with external candidates, or is there a complete internal process first before reaching out to external applicants?
> ➢ Where are you posting the job description?
> ➢ Are you being intentional about posting at outlets that have a diverse audience?
> ➢ Are candidates required to provide an equity statement, and is it weighed appropriately in the evaluation of the candidate?
> ➢ Are you explicit in your interview about your organization's commitment to race equity?
> ➢ Do the questions draw out the candidate's race equity fluency and competence? (I have included sample interview questions)

Phase IV – Ongoing Relationships

Our approach allows us to maintain ongoing dialogue and relationships that are instrumental in extending our recruitment efforts to diverse applicants. By taking this approach, we activate lifelong recruiters that may have access to applicants CLS has not reached. Our approach includes three steps: Job Fairs, Alumni Engagement, and an Open House Day with partner organizations.

We believe that by following these practices we will put ourselves in the best position to recruit and retain talented staff members who will bring new and innovative ways to serve our clients.

Purpose:

> ➤ Strengthens relationships and goodwill with allies and alum.
> ➤ Increases CLS visibility and establishes a diverse applicant pool through strategic recruitment efforts and ongoing relationship building/stewarding.

Questions to Ask:

> ➤ Is there a process in place to get feedback and capture the information of interns/externs/volunteers?
> ➤ Is there diverse representation at fairs and other outreach events?
> ➤ Are affinity groups encouraged to evangelize the work of the organization?
> ➤ Are there any events, newsletters or consistent touches that occur with alum and supporters?
> ➤ Once staff begin at CLS is there a process to successfully integrate them so that they are successful and want to keep ties with CLS?

When transforming an organization to be more inclusive and diverse, the hiring process becomes key in ensuring that this happens.

2. Professional Development

Staff of color raised concerns about the lack of opportunities to develop their skills, and that mentorship opportunities were often afforded to white staff. We used this as an opportunity to create a comprehensive mentorship program at CLS that would formally establish a pathway for all staff to broaden their talents and skills.

a. Mentorship Program

The goal of the CLS Mentorship Program is to improve the competence, professionalism, and health of new staff members. A dedicated mentor deepens the mentee's ability and capacity for professional thinking and problem solving; teaches the importance of civility and ethics; and serves as a resource in navigating new and difficult situations.

These goals are accomplished through the following objectives:

1. Provide professional development and support for new staff members within their first 3 years at Columbia Legal Services.

    a. Provide both personal and professional support for the mentee's professional development.

2. Enhance job satisfaction by providing opportunities for increased skill development:

    a. In the mentee's current position;
    b. To prepare the mentee for more diverse responsibilities; and
    c. To prepare the mentee for increased responsibilities.

3. Enhance performance, productivity and service to the organization, clients, communities served, and stakeholders.

Mentorship Program Implementation

Program Administrator

The Program Administrator for the Mentorship Program is the Equity Director. The Program Administrator is responsible for matching mentors with new mentees, organizing an orientation for the mentors and mentees, and collecting the mentoring agreements.

The Program Administrator may decide whether to do a mid-term program check to support the mentoring participants and to gain feedback on mentoring program development. Finally, to the extent extenuating circumstances prevent either mentor or mentee from completing the program or, if the mentoring relationship is not working, it is the responsibility of the Program Administrator to implement the procedures for reassignment of mentors and mentees.

Talent Bank: Selecting a Mentor

CLS has knowledge and skills within, and often outside of, the scope of their job. This knowledge and these skills can be shared with other employees' staff when needs arise. But these talents can't be tapped if no one knows about them.

CLS has a comprehensive Talent Bank that details the diverse skills and talents of our staff. A new staff member can obtain a mentor to develop skills such as writing, research, case planning, social media or other skills. Once the skill to be developed has been identified, the Program Administrator will search the Talent Bank for compatible skills and match the new staff member with a mentor.

Mentees

All new attorneys, legal assistants, and paralegals with less than 3 years of experience are encouraged to participate in the mentoring program. Attorneys, legal assistants, and paralegals with more than 3 years of experience are also welcome to become mentees when interested, and should contact the Program Administrator for assistance arranging the mentorship. An experienced staff member who joins CLS and may be new to legal aid may want to have a mentor and CLS will support this.

Mentors

The success of any mentoring program depends upon experienced and dedicated staff members who are willing to commit their time to serve as mentors so that they may personally convey the core values and best practices of the profession to less-experienced attorneys. To be effective, mentors should embrace sharing their knowledge and experience with mentees in the development of professional habits and strive to improve the legal profession through their mentorship. Mentors should have a minimum of 5 years' experience with CLS.

Mentors should possess interpersonal skills, an appreciation of the value of diversity in the practice of law, and have the ability to facilitate quality discussions about the best practices and highest values of the legal profession.

Program Orientation

The orientation is designed to provide the mentor and mentee with an overview of the mentoring program, clarify roles and expectations, and discuss how to handle a variety of situations. Participation in the orientation is mandatory.

The orientation will include an explanation and review of the activities and documentation that must be completed in order to satisfy the mentoring program. In addition, the orientation will address effective communication, problem-solving strategies, and the resources that are available to assist participants in achieving a successful mentoring relationship. Topics to be addressed in the orientation include:

1. Program goals
2. Mentoring relationship and term
3. Mentoring agreement, mentoring plan
4. Communication
5. Problem solving
6. Benefits and rewards of participation

Mentor and Mentee Responsibilities:

The first activity that the mentoring pair will participate in together is the orientation. Afterwards, the mentoring relationship is guided by a mutual agreement between the mentor and mentee. Terms of the relationship can be subject to adjustments/additions based on any special interests of the mentor and mentee.

At the end of the six-month formal mentoring term, mentors and mentees will complete a mentorship program evaluation and can choose informally to continue their mentor/mentee relationship.

At the end of the day, creating a mentorship program is a win-win-win. The mentee wins because they get the opportunity to grow and develop skills, the mentor wins because they get to not only develop skills as a leader, but the self-satisfaction of contributing to and making a difference for another, and the organization wins as it enjoys the benefit of establishing itself as a forward thinking organization that invests in the talent and development of its staff.

b. Performance Evaluations

Performance evaluations are one of the most misunderstood and underutilized communication tools an organization can use. Evaluations give managers the opportunity to recognize quality performance, while at the same time a formalized platform to have honest conversation about areas that need improvement.

The leadership/professional development team honed in on the confusion between, performance evaluations (PE), professional development (PD) and performance improvement plans (PIPs). CLS is one of many organizations that seems to get these three processes conflated. However, like many other organizations, CLS allowed staff to weigh in on these three performance mechanisms and create a way to clarify and streamline them.

So just to be sure we have a shared understanding of these three processes, here is a brief explanation.

- Performance Evaluations are an annual review of a staff members' performance including areas of strength and areas to develop as it relates to their assigned duties.
- Professional Development plans are staff driven goals that staff members would like to attain. As far as CLS was concerned, these were goals that were beyond the scope of their job description so there was no punitive measure if the PD wasn't met.
- Performance Improvement Plans are an intentional, time-bound plan that outlines specific steps a staff member must take in order to reach performance standards. It usually comes with an alternative consequence if the steps aren't taken or performance has not improved.

Here is what I've seen in a few nonprofits. Performance evaluations are conducted inconsistently. Add to that, a staff member cannot be disciplined/terminated unless they had a negative performance review. Therefore, when a manager wanted to let go of an employee, they would conduct a performance review. This led staff to associate performance reviews with termination, PIPs or some other disciplinary action.

Also, questions were raised about professional development goals being conflated with performance evaluations and whether or not there would be punitive actions taken if their professional development goals weren't met. The team wanted to ensure that all managers understood that performance evaluations were related to the duties outlined in their job description and that professional development goals were "above and beyond" these duties and should not have punitive outcomes if not met.

A final question was related to the inconsistencies between managers of why/how/when performance evaluations were conducted. These disparities among managers created inequitable conditions for staff.

This process gave leadership a chance to understand some of the mistrust by staff. It took more than a few weeks for leadership to work with our union to change the process and language in our Collective Bargaining Agreement (CBA) to ensure that there was clarity, consistency, and transparency related to how we handled the evaluation of all staff. Below are the changes:

- We separated Professional Development into its own section of the CBA to both literally and symbolically designate it as a separate process from Performance Evaluations.
- We created a public calendar for all staff to see when their performance reviews were coming. This held both manager and staff accountable for ensuring consistency of performance reviews.
- We committed to training all managers on our standardized process on conducting performance evaluations, as well as how to better provide coaching/mentorship related to professional development of teams.
- Finally, we changed language in our HR materials and CBA that indicated that a negative performance review is necessary before taking disciplinary action.

We understood that many of the concerns of staff stemmed from a time before this leadership team existed. We sometimes struggled with staff's lack of trust of leadership and felt we had to pay for mistakes that others made. But again, knowing that conflict and resistance is inherent in an organization, change of this level is inevitable and all that any leadership team can do is reinforce the message and keep pushing forward.

c. Trainings

Mandatory training requirements for all staff was mentioned as a solution in the Collective Letter. While we had an existing training calendar, it was mostly focused on advocacy related topics. The Office Culture team proposed that we supplement our existing calendar with topics that promoted the restorative culture we were committed to. So in addition to topics like, *"Bias & Racially Equitable Policy Advocacy"*, we added trainings such as *"Transparency and Safety"* and *"Bias, Race Equity, and Intersectionality"*. These monthly trainings are mandatory for all staff and are designed to equip our staff with the tools to better understand, communicate and engage with each other about race, race equity and our many perspectives. But ultimately, it makes us better equipped to serve and engage with our clients with a broadened perspective.

3. Advocacy

Race equity is at the heart of the work at CLS. Communities of color are disproportionately represented in racial inequities. Our advocacy work seeks to balance structural and enduring changes that increase the power of those who are disadvantaged politically, economically and socially and the race equity tool helps us achieve this change. Through our advocacy, we tackle the root and avoidable causes of inequities for those who are systematically and institutionally disadvantaged by their race and/or ethnicity. The work we've done internally has been in service of a strong commitment to our clients and communities we serve. To continue the fight of systemic racism without addressing our own organizational racist structures and culture, makes us co-conspirators in the existing arrangement that oppress those we serve.

a. Race Equity Tool

The race equity tool allows CLS to measure the impact that its advocacy has on the communities we serve, who we advocate with, how we collaborate, and what burden the affected communities will bear. The tool also allows us to judge and measure how race equity is integrated into our practice and process. This directly affects what advocacy we participate in and how we show up.

At the time of this writing, CLS was in the process of updating their Race Equity Tool Kit and therefore it is unavailable for this book. However, CLS has always positioned itself as an organization open and willing to sharing its resources. In the meantime, the following is the general idea of the Race Equity Tool Kit.

While CLS is a legal organization, I believe that all nonprofit or social justice organizations can evaluate their work/impact against the following six categories:

Category/Rationale	Sample Questions to Consider
Community Engagement: Advocates contribute their legal knowledge and skills to support initiatives identified by communities of color. Community directs the focus of this work.	Is this issue important to communities of color? How do you know? How was this issue identified? If it was not identified by the community, why not? What steps will we take to engage the community at each stage of the process including implementation and monitoring?

Systems Analysis: Race equity work can be most effective when it addresses the system as a whole.	What racialized systems are at issue? (examples: prisons, court systems, economic systems, foster care, health care, education, banking/credit, wage, etc.) How will you work within that system and not perpetuate structural or institutional racism?
Advocacy Goals and Objectives: Identifies the most effective ways to change or interrupt processes that create racial inequity.	What racial disparities does the group or community want to eliminate, reduce or prevent? How will the community's or group's position be changed or be the same in the system as a result of this advocacy? Will they have more positional power? If the advocacy you want to undertake is successful, what is the best possible outcome you can envision?
Implicit/Explicit Racism: Identifies the type(s) of racism the work seeks to address. (Personal, internalized, interpersonal, institutional, structural)	What factors may be producing and perpetuating racial inequities associated with this issue? How did the inequities arise? What data resources do you need? How will you obtain them?
Data: Research and analyze the quantitative and qualitative evidence of inequities for this advocacy. Consider what information is missing that you might need.	What factors may be producing and perpetuating racial inequities associated with this issue? How did the inequities arise? What data resources do you need? How will you measure your work?
Messaging: Creating strong, values-based narrative that can change the larger national conversation, shift the culture, and result in lasting change.	What are the **values** behind your program goals? How are you talking about your organization, clients, etc.? What is the **problem** you are addressing? What is the **solution** you propose? What **action** should people take? How can you talk about race in your messaging?

What's Next for CLS?

CLS continues to grow and evolve. The internal work of race equity will continue.

Now is the time for CLS to "take it to the streets". In other words, being more focused on integrating race equity into advocacy and community relationships. The next iteration of the Equity Director role will likely include working more closely with the Advocacy Director to examine current practices related to community engagement/community lawyering and ensuring that CLS's external work aligns to its internal agreements and values.

Travis Andrews is now CLS's Equity Director and he holds great hope and enthusiasm for the future. Following are his reflections.

Michelle: So you've been on this journey for a while. When did you come in to the Equity Team?

Travis: I joined the Equity Team in August of 2017.

Michelle: And during that time, what has been your experience?

Travis: Well, there were a number of things that I worked on and helped with, one being like the hiring practices and how we recruit, who we recruit and where we're recruiting. All of those things play a factor into who ends up in this organization. Also how we handle conflict, stepping away from the punitive models and stepping into a place where we are calling people *in* versus calling people *out*. So creating opportunities for people to be able to process things in a group setting, where they're not just dealing with their own version of what happened, but also what others may have experienced as well.

I've also been involved in thinking through how we engage as an organization. That really impacts how we show up in our work. So being intentional in the way that we interact with each other on a much more personal level has transformed the way that we see each other, how we engage, our willingness to be vulnerable in certain settings. All of that has been a major factor and some of the things that I've seen having been a part of that.

Michelle: So, as a person who has stepped into this role, as Equity Director of Columbia Legal Services, what are some of the things you've learned so far that for sure you're going to take with you?

Travis: There are a couple of things. I think one is how we engage communities and what communities we engage with. It's one thing that I think equity has to be present in those. The other is the politics around community. So not just who we're engaging with but also why we're engaging with these groups. The community politics can be just as, if not more, complicated than the legislature. So I think how we engage in those communities can be very valuable to how we show up in our work.

The last thing is how equity shows up in our attitude. How are we choosing our projects and how are we approaching our projects? I know that we identify ourselves as community-led *advocates,* but what does that mean? What is community? How do we find ourselves interacting with community? Are we separate from community? Do we go into community? Are we a part of the community working from the inside? Those things are, I think, very important questions that need to be answered and addressed. I think we're in a very good position. I think Michelle, you've left us in the perfect spot in transitioning to that external realm and how equity plays a role in that.

Michelle: So, what are you most excited about this new role - in particular for your own personal growth and development?

Travis: For my own personal growth and development, I think specifically how equity shows up in our advocacy. That's the development piece because I approach my work using an *advocacy lens* and I also use an *equity lens* but very rarely do I have that opportunity to combine those two things as intentionally as I can now. So I'm really excited to develop more in my capacity to bring these things together as one and how to function within that.

One of the things that I know that CLS needs is a streamlined community engagement model. Everybody has their own thing and I think individually people do great work. But it will be great to see or have something that we can use as something tangible, that we can all refer to, whether you have the strengths in that area or not. To have something streamlined for that process will be great. That's something I'm really excited about.

Michelle: As you know, this book is for leaders, nonprofits, and other justice organizations. For the person reading this book with an interest in doing race equity work, what would you say to them to be prepared for?

Travis: Yeah. I think one thing that comes to mind is it's going to get very uncomfortable. If you do not want to be uncomfortable, then you probably don't want to approach this work.

It is very difficult to sit individuals down or to galvanize an organization of individuals around a subject matter that has been taboo for the existence of our country. We are at a place now where we can address these things and we can do it in a very productive way.

So that is going to come with discomfort. So I would say just be aware of that Now, I know this is going to sound trite, but trust the process. It's going to be uncomfortable. It's going to get difficult. Stick to it and trust the process. Trust what you do. That's what I will say.

III

Reflections

I learned so much throughout this process. As a result of this work at CLS, I have moved into the world of consulting only to find other organizations grappling with the same issues of uncertainty, frustration, but commitment to do this work. Here are some of the key takeaways that I bring to my clients:

Don't be shy about hiring and promoting staff who are highly fluent and experienced in their understanding of race equity issues. When you are doing the depth of work that CLS has been doing, individuals who are keen and experienced in race equity work should be required, not just "strongly desired". I've seen the effects on morale when people in key positions aren't as astute in the issues of race equity. It really does undermine the leaders' vision and erodes trust of staff. The leaders MUST be vocal and explicit about this commitment – leaving no room for it as an option. CLS actually has its own race equity orientation for new hires.

Put your money where your values are. If you want to know what an organization values, just track where they invest their money. CLS deployed considerable financial resources to make sure that we were able to carry out the work and vision of #OneCLS. Many organizations don't have the same resources as CLS, and may have to stretch themselves, but whatever that "stretch" dollar figure is for your organization, allocate it.

Be vigilant about who is at the decision-making table. We had a diverse leadership team. Diverse in tenure, race, gender, identity, neuro-diversity (how we processed and thought things through) socioeconomic status and organizational priorities. Because of this, we were considerably more equipped to account for the concerns of staff, and in particular staff of color, who are often left out of the process. For example, there were some decisions that I thought should be "simple" to make. But after factoring in the diversity of our leadership team and the range of perspectives and priorities we each held, conversations became more complex. While this made it more challenging and time consuming to come to decisions at some points, we could at least say that between the seven of us, the interests of the staff were more accurately represented.

Staying the course. I have a colleague who is working with an organization who entered this work with an overly simplistic view and when things got rough, not only did the organization implode, but the leader folded under the pressure and left the organization, without notice, or a plan for the organization to move forward. The only board member who could step in had no race equity experience or proficiency and people begin to leave. The moral of the story is to plan for the resistance and stay the course. Let everyone know that you are staying the course, and steel your resolve for those moments when things get tense.

The most important thing I can say is focus on relationship building of staff. Race work is "social" and "heart" work. It requires patience, forgiveness, support and courage. All of these require a safe space. People mostly feel safe with those with whom they have a relationship with. All of this takes time, which is why you have to stay the course.

In Closing

There were times over the past three years, where I so, so deeply regretted ever agreeing to this role. My emotions were all over the place. I felt rage at yet another black man killed by police, which would translate into deep resentment about why I had to work so hard for my white co-workers to move past their "discomfort" to even talk about race. There were times that I felt resentment toward staff of color as well. Being part of the leadership team gave me access to information and I was clear about how much staff of color's concerns were considered. So when I sensed The Collective's impatience, frustration or lack of gratitude, I would be incensed. I also resented our leadership team at times when I felt we weren't moving fast enough on issues that were causing people to make assumptions or become disgruntled. But, I learned that there were just times where there were so many moving parts that we had to make decisions to be "still" rather than jump ahead of the optics.

Finally, I battled with my own dragons. The first thing I needed to learn was not to take things personally. OH MY GOD did I take things personally. I was charged with a body of work that staff sometimes resented having to do. I interpreted that to mean they resented *me*. All of my insecurities have been having a field day over the past few years, constantly reminding me, "Girlfriend, you are not the one who should be doing this work".

My saving grace was that somewhere along the way, I was able to make that separation between being "attached" versus being "committed" to the vision for this work at CLS. I'm not quite sure why or when it happened, but this was when I was able to have more compassion for myself and others, realizing that race may never (in my lifetime) be an easy subject for anyone. We all feel like we are screwing it up or fear we will, and we all are struggling to find ourselves in the ridiculous system that we were born into.

One of the greatest gifts I took away from grad school is consistently doing the work of striking a balance between these three leadership worlds:

1. **Leadership of myself**

   a. Goal: Stay true to my core values
   b. My challenge: Being concerned about what others think/ beating up on myself
   c. Impact: Affects my ability to motivate and inspire people

2. **Leadership of Others**

   a. Goal: Understand and connect with others
   b. My challenge: Not taking things personally
   c. Impact: Affects my ability to bring out the best in them and myself

3. **Leadership in systems and organizations**

   a. Goal: Understand big picture systems and structures
   b. My challenge: Putting smaller parts in bigger organizational context
   c. Impact: Affects my ability to see how my smaller actions affect bigger vision

The idea is for a leader to be able to integrate these three worlds. I have always been most comfortable in leading myself and others, but my work at CLS has taught me how tricky things can be in leading at the level of an organization. For example, in my role as Equity Director, I was most concerned with the people and their experience. Are they happy? Do they have what they need? Are their concerns being heard and addressed? Others on our leadership team were most concerned about organizational efficiency. "This is a business", "Does it make financial sense to invest in this?" "Is it a good idea to take people away from advocacy work to attend that?"

Another example is when doing our Restorative Justice work. The language and spirit of Restorative Justice principles are centered on being accountable for mistakes made on both the part of the organization and the individual. It was about owning mistakes, and addressing any harm experienced. You can imagine in a law office how many people had strong reactions about admitting any wrongdoing and especially using words like, "harm". So we had to find the sweet spot where we could still do the work of Restorative Justice while being legally responsible, for example using words like "impact" versus "harm".

Race equity work isn't really efficient. Nor is really fun. Racism is upheld by a multi-dimensional, complex and *deliberate* arrangement designed to keep people distracted, afraid and too exhausted to fight. This arrangement also keeps people from demanding more from our government, each other and ourselves. To do this work requires an almost irrational faith in the human spirit. Despite what is going on in our nation and world, I applaud CLS for continuing the fight for justice for each other, and its relentless pursuit of justice for the clients they serve.

T H E   E N D

Resources

"Awake to Woke, to Work." https://www.bridgespan.org/bridgespan/Images/articles/role-senior-leaders-building-race-equity-culture/ProInspire-Equity-in-Center-publication-digital-July-2018.pdf

"How to Develop and Support Leadership that Contributes to Racial Justice." July 2010. http://www.racialequitytools.org/resourcefiles/keleher2.pdf

Race Equity Tools: http://www.racialequitytools.org/act/strategies/leadership-development

Research on the racial leadership gap http://racetolead.org/

Transforming culture - An examination of workplace values through the frame of white dominant culture", for Management Information Exchange in the spring 2018 issue and published by the MIE Journal on www.mielegalaid.org.

"What are Your Values? Deciding What's Most Important in Life." https://www.mindtools.com/pages/article/newTED_85.htm

"White Privilege." *Putting Racism on the Table*, www.puttingracismonthetable.org/copy-of-john-powell.

"Workplace Conflict and How Businesses Can Harness It to Thrive Global Human Capital." Report CPP2008. Available at: https://www.cpp.com/pdfs/CPP Global Human Capital Report Workplace Conflict.pdf

Made in the USA
Lexington, KY
03 December 2018